FORMERLY A WIFE

FORMERLY A Wife

*A survival guide for women
facing the pain and disruption of divorce*

WELBY O'BRIEN

WingSpread Publishers
Camp Hill, Pennsylvania

WingSpread Publishers

3825 Hartzdale Drive · Camp Hill, PA 17011
www.wingspreadpublishers.com

A division of Zur Ltd.

Formerly a Wife
ISBN: 978-1-60066-176-1
LOC Control Number: 2007929344
© 1996 by Welby O'Brien

Previously published by Christian Publications, Inc.
First Christian Publications Edition 1996
First WingSpread Publishers Edition 2007

11   10   09   08   07   5   4   3   2   1

Welby O'Brien is available for
conferences and special events.
www.welbyo.com
(503) 254-8157

With thanks to the Lord
for His love, for
Mom, Dad, Bobby and Kevin

Contents

Introduction

From One Who's Been There

"Congratulations" would not necessarily be my first choice of words to you, but rather, "Welcome. You are not alone." You never dreamed it would happen to you, but you are now an official "ex-wife." Be encouraged to know you are not the first nor will you be the last.

As a recent ex-wife myself, I felt like I was the first and *only* one who was in my situation. Most of my primary supporters were married Christians. With their help, I had to take each day as it came and handle each situation the best I knew how.

Looking back, I would have greatly valued the support, encouragement, empathy and wisdom of someone who had *been there herself*.

The threefold purpose of this book is to help you take comfort in knowing you are not alone and what you are experiencing is not uncommon; to help you be prepared for the bumps that may be ahead in your road; and to help you take those next few steps as a newly divorced woman.

Although it may not be by your choice that you are where you are today, you can begin now by becoming an active choice maker in each of the situations that come your way.

The first chapter addresses some vital areas that will equip you to handle the uncharted territory of your redirected life.

The remaining chapters delve into the typical day-to-day issues facing a newly divorced woman. Since every woman is unique, every ex-husband is

unique, and every situation is unique, all the ex-
amples may not match your situation, but the
principles will hold their value.

I have chosen to write this book under my
maiden name for legal and personal reasons. The
names of my son, my ex-husband and his new
wife, as well as the names of other divorced
women in Appendix A have been changed to protect their identity.

My prayer for you as you read this book is that
you will release yourself to feel the feelings as certain issues hit home and that you will also seize
your God-given ability to make wise choices as
opportunities arise.

Chapter 1

Checklist for Survival

Thursday, the 6th

When I look to You, Lord, faith just comes naturally.

When I look at my circumstances, You seem far away and not very powerful.

Keep my eyes on You, Lord.

Steve and I both came from decent homes where both sets of parents have been married over thirty-five years. We met at a Christian college, fell in love and were married following graduation. We were always best friends, and it was probably that friendship that kept us together for thirteen years.

He worked as a youth pastor and then went on to seminary to become a counselor, while I spent many years teaching. We were always active in Christian ministry, had a good social life and got along well. It's likely that many were envious of our marriage.

But none of us is perfect. I had my faults, immaturities and weaknesses, and so did Steve. We did our best to work through problems as they arose.

Eight and a half years into our marriage, Danny was born. What a special blessing! But somehow, at some point in time, Steve began withdrawing from me. I don't know if it was denial on my part, or maybe the distractions of motherhood, but I didn't see it as a serious concern.

A few years later, Steve and I had a couple of major conflicts one of which, I found out later, he never got over.

After those conflicts were seemingly resolved, we were again—I thought—working through the issues as they arose and going on.

When he informed me on December 3rd that he no longer wanted to be married, I was shocked.

Three weeks later he moved out. (Merry Christmas!)

And it wasn't long until he was spending nights with her.

The next year and a half was a blur of anger, manipulation and threats from Steve, attorneys, attorney fees, insomnia, health problems, fear and an emotionally distraught little boy—my world as I knew it was being ripped out from under me. I could do nothing to stop it.

Today things have stabilized, my life continues and I feel good. What took place in between then and now is what lies ahead in this book.

I have talked with many women and listened to them share their stories. No two are exactly alike. Some have been physically or emotionally abused. Some have been betrayed or abandoned. Some women themselves have left or initiated the divorce.

Whatever the circumstances, none of us is perfect. None of us has always made all the right choices. And perhaps none of us can fully understand what each other is going through.

Yet we all share something in common: Each of us is hurting over the broken relationship. Happily ever after will never be. Rather, we've experienced the death of a relationship. The death of a lifelong dream.

The feelings which overwhelm us may be a mixture of hatred, hopelessness, fear, betrayal, abandonment, anger, disillusionment, depression, relief, pessimism, fright, worthlessness, guilt, panic, exhaustion, suicidal thoughts, revenge, helplessness, loneliness and grief. We know first-hand why God hates divorce—not with a head knowledge of theological assent, but with the pain of personal experience. God knows what divorce does to its victims.

From this point on, each of us will proceed on her own timetable of recovery. The circumstances, available choices and makeup of each individual will affect that rate of survival, healing and, ultimately, growth.

As you go through the routine of your normal daily activities, you may have a pointless, uneventful day or you may encounter a divorce-related issue. In the upward spiral of the growth process, I have found that I do best when I've taken care of myself. I've also learned that if I don't take care of myself, I can't rely on any other human to do it. The following list of fifteen things have become part of my life and are in place both for daily maintenance and for unexpected bumps in the road.

☐ 1. *Saturate yourself with Scripture.* Everybody is at a different level in his or her walk with the Lord. In my times of deep pain, I soaked up Scripture and leaned on the promises of comfort throughout the day. Passages I'd known for years suddenly took on a deep reality. When verses met my needs at certain times, I wrote them on cards and posted them on the refrigerator and other places to remind me to refocus. The more my mind was on the Lord and His eternal perspective, the easier it was to go on. For some humanly unexplainable reason, the Word of God provides comfort and power when we choose to fill our crumbling, aching soul with it.

☐ 2. *Pour out your heart to God.* I need to keep the lines of communication open with my Shepherd, my Creator, my Provider. Regardless of the need I am feeling, I try to relate that need to an attribute of God. When I feel weak, I remember He is all-powerful. I tell Him of my failing spirit and beg Him for strength. When I feel like a helpless little girl, I come to Him as my daddy, climbing into His lap as I pour out my heart and let the tears flow. I cry out for His tenderness, love and comfort. When I am consumed by hatred and anger and want to strike out in revenge, I come to Him demanding that He pay back to Steve the wickedness and destruction he deserves. I remember God is not only just but also patient. Sometimes I am angry at God Himself for allowing this unfairness. I remember God is forgiving. I can always unload, always cry out and never have to pretend. He hears. He cares.

☐ 3. *Feel the pain.* This is not a time to ignore feelings. As at any other time in life, feelings don't just go away, much less the overwhelming, intense range of emotions that flood a person during and after divorce. As humans, our natural instinct is to avoid pain or stop it as soon as possible. Physical pain was designed to alert us to illness or injury and prompts us to either stop what is causing it or to take steps to promote healing.

Likewise, with emotional pain, we often try to squelch it any way we can. Emotional pain, like physical pain, is an indicator of a wound or illness that needs attention.

Denial is a term used to describe how we try to cover up our unwanted feelings with something that distracts or brings temporary pleasure. I have had to retrain myself when I encounter pain to pause and consciously urge myself to be aware of it. To let it hurt. To not turn on the TV or start eating. The healing begins with the acknowledgement of pain. It continues as I provide healthy outlets for the feelings I consciously process (talking, praying, writing, crying, running, etc.). Pruning my bushes was one of my quickest, most satisfying outlets for anger. (The neighbors could always tell how things were going by looking at my yard. It's amazing that there's anything living left standing!)

Allow yourself the freedom to acknowledge, identify, feel and accept each feeling, and from there decide the healthiest way to deal with it.

☐ 4. *Let yourself cry.* If I had a dollar for each cupful of tears I shed in the last two years, I could put a dent in the federal deficit. I used to try to save my tears in order to release them when I was by myself, but that didn't work for long. I cried in the car, on the telephone, in the grocery store, at the gym and always at church. Some days I knew I needed to cry and couldn't. Then something triggered the release, a weight was lifted and the peace of exhaustion settled inside me. It's OK to cry. It's necessary to cry. It's healthy to cry.

☐ 5. *Talk to someone trustworthy.* Thankfully, the Lord surrounded me with many friends and from those I chose a select few I could trust. My mother and I have always been close, so she bore my burden as I told her everything. I have two close friends with whom I also shared many of my ups and downs. And as the circle of friends got broader, I decided who heard what. I recognized my need to talk as a cleansing process and also a decision-making process. Talking to a close friend or a professional counselor who cares is a healthy way to release your burden as well as to work through the situation at hand.

☐ 6. *Laugh, giggle, play.* Thousands of years ago, the author of Proverbs wrote that a merry heart is medicinal (Proverbs 17:22). Now modern medical science is finally admitting the physical benefit of laughter, among which is the release of the tranquilizing hormones called endorphins. Laughter helps lighten the load and renew perspective. Some of my best therapy occurred when I allowed the child in me to play. Just be careful not to use laughter as a cover-up for the pain or a wall of defense to hide behind. Don't force it, but give it opportunity. It feels so good and is one step closer to healing.

☐ 7. *Be open to wise input.* You will find you are hungry to learn about this strange phenomenon of divorce. There will be many "whys" for which you'll seek answers. Take advantage of this opportunity to fill your mind with godly books, tapes and music. Like taking vitamins, this constructive input will strengthen you and equip you during this intense phase of growth.

☐ 8. *Write down your feelings.* I never had the discipline or saw the value of keeping a journal until I came to this time in my life where I needed an outlet. My thoughts and feelings accumulated and intermingled during the day, so that by nighttime I needed to sort through them. As I wrote, things became clearer, and at the same time I felt relieved of the garbage that had stacked up throughout the day. The Psalms are an example to us of how a godly man used writing to pour out his heart to the Lord.

☐ 9. *Make sleep a priority.* This is essential for facing the challenges of each day, both physically and emotionally. Easier said than done when your mind and emotions are in turmoil. I finally put in a call to my doctor when I realized I couldn't handle it on my own. He recommended some mild sleeping pills as a temporary solution. As circumstances eased and my emotions became more even keeled, I didn't need them any more. Whatever you find to be the healthiest way to get it, be sure to place a high priority on sleep.

☐ 10. *Fill your body with healthy things.* The best part of the divorce was the weight I lost near the beginning. I was in such turmoil, I couldn't eat. (Not a recommended way to lose weight!) I also became run down, and my immune system was not able to keep up. Although I couldn't control my circumstances, at least I could do my best to fortify the fortress. Extra B vitamins, calcium, magnesium, vitamins C, A and E have become part of my life. In addition, I attempted to make sure each thing I ate and and drank had nutritional value.

☐ 11. *Do some physical activity every day.* This is a wonderful way to get rid of pent-up anger and to release endorphins which can tremendously improve perspective. Choose an enjoyable form of exercise. If it's not enjoyable, it will become another stress. If it is something you look forward to, it will be a treat, and you will keep at it. My two favorite outlets were walking alone with my dog and playing racquetball with my good friends.

☐ 12. *Be your best.* From the inside out, we need to be our best, do our best and look our best. It's a full circle, originating from within by knowing and accepting who we are in God's sight and continuing to the external manifestation of all we do.

It's a choice of playing the role of a victim and having an extended pity party or learning to be victorious. When we take those extra steps to fix our hair and makeup, dress nicely, keep the house clean and fulfill our responsibilities at work and home, it's worth it. If I don't feel good before I make these choices, I usually feel great *after*. Though we may have every right to feel sorry for ourselves, we have to come to the point where we pick up and go on to be the best we can be.

☐ 13. *Treat yourself.* I've always felt guilty doing something just for myself and especially now as finances are tighter. Yet I need to remind myself that I am special, and if I don't nurture myself, no one else will. So I've given myself permission to splurge occasionally: buy a flowering plant, enjoy new bubble bath, rent a video, stop for a frozen yogurt cone, buy new underwear, use the pretty dishes or get a massage. I am also realizing the importance of time alone. Even Jesus took time out.

☐ 14. *Let go.* Whatever it is that is holding you back, keeping you from growing and going on with your life, let it go. For some it may be anger, bitterness or inability to forgive. Others may be tenaciously gripping the hope that their ex-husbands will change and the marriage will be restored. For me it was the issue of fairness. I had to realize and accept the fact that divorce is never fair, and nobody wins. It is easy to allow an obsession to cripple us and to squeeze out our remaining energy. Letting go does not deny that the problem exists, nor does it require the particular solution we'd most like to see. It just frees us from the physical, spiritual and emotional erosion of worry. Letting go acknowledges that the situation is out of our control and in the hands of One whose knowledge of the situation and love for me is beyond comprehension.

☐ 15. *Don't rush.* Our tendency as humans is to try to hurriedly get through the pain so we can resume a comfortable life. Look at this trial not as a detour or a mistake, but as *the plan*—His plan. God has something beautiful to do in your life through this ugly and seemingly destructive situation. Wait on Him. Trust. Expect good things. Let time work for you.

Scriptures

1. Saturate yourself with Scripture.
> Psalm 119:25, 71, 116, 144, 165
> 2 Timothy 3:15-17

2. Pour out your heart to God.
> Psalm 143:5, 8
> Psalm 145:14-21
> Philippians 4:6-7
> 1 Thessalonians 5:17
> 1 Peter 5:7

3. Feel the pain.

Psalm 69:16-20; 29-30
Psalm 71:14-21
Romans 8:26-27
Hebrews 4:15

4. Let yourself cry.

Psalm 61:1-4
Psalm 120:1
Psalm 126:5-6
Isaiah 38:14

5. Talk to someone trustworthy.

Psalm 55:12-14
Galatians 6:2

6. Laugh, giggle, play.

Nehemiah 8:10
Proverbs 17:22
1 Thessalonians 5:16

7. Be open to wise input.

Psalm 119:99
Proverbs 12:25; 13:20
Philippians 4:8-9
Colossians 3:16

8. Write down your feelings.

Nehemiah 8:7-10
The Psalms

9. Make sleep a priority.
>   Psalm 23:1-3
>   Matthew 11:28-30
>   Mark 6:31

10. Fill your body with healthy things.
>   Daniel 1:8
>   Romans 12:1
>   1 Corinthians 6:19-20

11. Do some physical activity every day.
>   Romans 12:1
>   1 Corinthians 6:19-20
>   1 Timothy 4:8

12. Be your best.
>   Colossians 3:23
>   Hebrews 12:1
>   1 Peter 3:3-4

13. Treat yourself.
>   Luke 4:42
>   Luke 6:12
>   Luke 10:38-42

14. Let go.
>   Deuteronomy 33:27
>   Isaiah 30:15
>   Isaiah 40
>   Romans 11:33-36
>   Philippians 3:12-14

15. *Don't rush.*

> Psalm 37
> Romans 8:28

Reflection:

1. Rate yourself on each of the survival items listed in this chapter:

   A = Terrific
   B = OK
   C = Needs Help

2. List three things you can do to boost your level of survival.

   Today I choose to:

   _____

   Tomorrow I also choose to:

   _____

   The next day I also choose to:

   _____

3. With whom can you share this? Who will support and encourage you to keep up the good work?

Chapter 2

You: The Ex-Wife

Monday, the 22nd

Lord, keep my heart open to You and tender so I may love and feel. But help me be strong, to go on, to protect and provide.

Wednesday, the 5th

Long ride home after massage—ahhh! Sang "You Are My Hiding Place," then lots of praises.

God is so good! Why does it take pain to realize how wonderful our God is? I guess that's because we're human.

The divorce is final. Who am I now? What am I worth? The one person who knew me best and loved me most has rejected me. People say they care, but they're busy dealing with their own problems. Yes, I know that God loves me and Jesus died for me, but how does that translate to my pain, my needs and my value today?

I wrestled with these questions over and over. I have finally come to believe and feel some conclusions as a result of this process. When we start with the truth of God's Word, work through it and talk through it, add input from godly people and change some of the negative thought patterns we've developed about ourselves, then the biblical concepts become reality.

If, during marriage, we allowed our value to be based on being wives, now we must rebuild. If, during marriage, we developed a healthy sense of who we are and became involved in things we do well which are not necessarily tied to our husbands, then our task is not as overwhelming. My whole life was not devastated because I had through the years developed a sense of who I was and did a variety of things independently of my husband.

But even so, I had to struggle with my new identity as an ex-wife. At times I questioned my worth. No matter how intense this issue is for you, the answer always comes back to the ultimate truth: We are valuable because God made us in His image and then redeemed us through the blood of Jesus Christ.

There are many excellent books on self-esteem. But even after reading them we must release the erroneous thought that our worth went out the door with our former husbands. Fill that void with the reality that *you are* special. Your ex-husband's opinion does *not* determine your worth. We need to look to the ultimate opinion: the Creator of the universe (and incidently, the Creator of your ex-husband).

A major application of this truth for me has been in the area of choice making. I have always been comfortable in a somewhat dependent role where I can voice my opinion but don't have to make decisions. When I married, I transferred my tendency to rely on the decisions of my parents to my husband. Suddenly on my own, I was thrust into a world which daily demanded that I make choices. I had to choose what type of oil to put in my car as well as who should have the authority in my will to turn off life support if necessary.

Two realizations have been key to freeing me to make decisions more confidently: First, I am not perfect, and though I try my best, I will make mistakes. That is OK. Second, if I don't take care of myself, I can't rely on any other human to do it. My new responsibility is to survive and to take care of my family. As long as I am accomplishing that in the Lord's strength and with His wisdom, all the other things are incidental.

I faced several challenges in developing my new identity.

1. Am I less of a person than I was before?

I had no husband. I could no longer boast a diamond on my left hand. I still got mail addressed to Mr. and Mrs. "Smith." There is no Mr. here, and am I still a "Mrs."? Or am I a "Ms."? People asked me if I was going to change back to my maiden name. How was I to know?

Well, I made some adjustments, and I made some choices. I got to the point where "Mr. and Mrs." didn't bother me. People who improperly addressed my mail did it out of ignorance (mostly junk mail), and to the ones that really mattered I requested a change. I may go back to my maiden name someday, especially if it looks like I won't be remarrying. But for now, I chose to keep my married surname for two reasons. The first reason is because I have a son. Not long ago he complained about not liking his last name. Even if this is a normal phase for all children, that would not have been a good time for me to change my name. Keeping the same name reinforces our bond and gives security to him as well as simplifying matters that require my signature. It also may alleviate some pressures in certain social situations. The second reason is because my married name is the one by which everybody in my current world knows me. It would be a major disruption to my already fragile identity to have a name change also.

I treated myself to several new rings (from a wholesale catalog) and got used to wearing them

on my right hand. I do long for the day when I
can wear a diamond on my left hand again, but
only when it is symbolic of a healthy, God-cen-
tered marriage. And it's OK for me to feel a sting
when I see other women (presumably happily
married) with beautiful rings. Maybe I'll never
have that privilege again, but I am choosing not to
feel sorry for myself.

My value comes from within. I am a beautiful,
godly woman, and I am learning to understand
how priceless that is. I am learning not to place the
verdict of my value in the hands of any human ju-
ror but to accept the final ruling from the highest
Judge Himself.

*2. Is there something wrong with the way I look, and
what should I do about it?*

"It's obvious I am too fat, too wrinkled, too
short. Maybe I have been dressing like a slob
around the house too much. I should try a shorter
hairstyle. Any idiot would conclude that if I
looked more attractive I'd still have a husband."

I remember one day I looked closely in a mag-
nifying mirror. I was horrified to see nose hairs.
My immediate assumption was that if only I had
noticed those earlier I could have done something
about it and possibly prevented my divorce.
Could I have a second chance?

If you think such thoughts, join the club. Faulty
conclusions like these are a normal result of pressure
from our culture and possibly our upbringing.

Here's the situation: You're probably kicking yourself for all the "I should have" items, wondering if your looks are to blame for your divorce. You are also probably evaluating your looks because now you are single and "on the market." Whether or not you have deliberately "advertised," it is a fact.

I felt so exposed at this realization. All along I could hide behind a loving, accepting, committed husband. Or so I thought. Nobody wants used furniture that looks used, but some people might be willing to buy it if it was reupholstered. So, how do you look? What are your selling points? Do you need some reupholstery?

Now it's time to make a choice. Based on who you are on the inside and how God sees your ultimate worth, what do you want to do about the outside? The secret is to reupholster only the areas *you* want to, because *you* want to, not because you think you should. Try to make your external appearance *reflect* your inside worth rather than *dictate* it.

I chose to wear the same hairstyle and let the gray keep on coming. I have become consistent in using sunscreen whether or not I have a man to appreciate my skin—I like nice skin. I'll be living in this skin until the Lord takes me home. I have become even more conscious of proper eating habits and am at the point where I look forward to my regular exercise sessions. It feels good to be in shape, whether or not I am "on the market."

And then there are the things over which I have no control. I am learning to let go, not to beat myself, and to say, "Yep, this is the way my body is, and *I am OK*." Cellulite? Sagging chest and butt? Ever-increasing wrinkles? I even noticed the beginning of a double chin the other day! And the list goes on.

On the flip side, I enjoy my features that *are* attractive, being careful not to place my worth in them and guarding against pride.

"I am me, and I am OK." Get used to saying that. It's true!

3. Was I a lousy wife, and which of my character flaws needs the most attention?

There's a healthy balance between the one extreme of believing every negative thing you hear and think about yourself and the other extreme of thinking you are perfect. I had to listen honestly to my former husband's criticisms, sort through them and choose which to believe and which to trash. Because divorce always involves two humans, no one person is ever 100 percent at fault or 100 percent perfect.

My tendency was to believe the garbage he dumped on me and to seriously question my worth as a wife. Probably the most valuable route for me was to bounce these questions off those who really knew me. It was a wonderful way to objectively deal with the self-doubts.

It is a process, and I still struggle at times, yet

the self-imposed guilt has been lifted. Now I feel more confident and am free to take an honest look at the areas that really *can* stand some improvement. This is the place where normal, healthy, growing Christians have to be to become all that God wants them to be. Humbly acknowledge your weaknesses, accept God's unconditional love for you and ask Him to show you where you need to grow. (I always add a P.S. to these prayers, asking God to show me one thing at a time and to work in me to bring about the change.)

I get into trouble when I start comparing myself with other people. One of the traps I fell into frequently was to observe, with a twinge of envy and cynicism, other women who were still married. I wondered what *they* had that I didn't. I felt like marching up to the husband, getting in his face and asking, "Don't you think *I'd* make a good wife? What does *she* have that makes you stick around?"

I finally realized that everyone is unique, every marriage is different. The reasons they stay married or split up had *no* bearing on who I was or what kind of wife I had been. My ex-husband has an opinion about me, but even that does not necessarily reflect the truth.

I encourage you to listen to the criticisms (once is enough), pray for wisdom, talk to close friends or a counselor, sort through it all and make a choice. Discard that which is false and be open to growth in the areas that need improvement. Then, periodically, look back and feel thankful for your progress.

4. How do I deal with this sudden loneliness?

There's no one next to you in bed anymore. Why bother going out to eat or to the movies? There's no one to come home to after work. No one to share the good and the bad. After the kids are in bed, it's just me and the Lord. Compounded with feelings of rejection and abandonment, loneliness can be a painful ache. It never completely goes away, and at times it seems to penetrate to a depth you never knew you had.

Everyone will experience loneliness at different times and in varying degrees. Here again is another opportunity to honestly feel the pain and then to decide what to do about it.

I did not experience loneliness as intensely as others have. Ironically, I've often felt guilty about that. I've received lots of well-intentioned sympathy that I don't deserve. To be honest, solitude is one of the few things I appreciate.

Personality combined with perspective influences our view of aloneness. I have always enjoyed my space, my independence and time alone (to a certain degree). On the other hand many women feel a constant need to be with others. Those are the women who will experience the pain of loneliness to a greater degree.

As for perspective, there may be two ways to view the situation, and this is where choice is in-

volved. You can claim desertion and all of the unfairness that comes with it, or you can proclaim,
"Alone at last!" Loneliness can become solitude,
something many people consider a privilege. We
can choose to pity ourselves as victims, or we can
welcome time alone as an opportunity to relax, to
develop our inner self and deepen our relationship
with God.

You and I no longer have a marriage companion, and it hurts. But we now have the decision
either to wallow in our grief or to thrive. With a
healthy mind-set, we can be more open to various
social opportunities and may even find that to be
fun!

5. *How do I get my physical needs met without sinning?*

For twelve years, I had the God-given luxury
and freedom to enjoy sex anytime (with Steve, of
course). Now suddenly, the sensual smorgasbord
is off limits, and according to Scripture, I have
been put on an indefinite "fast." Sometimes I get
very hungry.

Our range of physical needs extends beyond the
sexual act itself, which of course is not an option
for divorced Christian women desiring God's will.
As we all know there are other alternatives, but in
the absence of a man you love there remains a
void. (There are many excellent resources available in this area. See Appendix D.)

Feeling so vulnerable, both physically and emotionally, can drive some of us who are recently di-

vorced into the arms of the nearest man who
shows even the slightest bit of interest. When we
were sixteen and told we were too young for marriage or motherhood, we may not have believed it.
Similarly, at this point in life, it's dangerous to
jump into another relationship. And that's the last
thing you want to hear. But I encourage you to
wait. With every day that passes, you'll become
stronger and wiser, and your ability to make the
best choices will increase.

As in any other challenge, the first step is to
be aware of the need. It was at church that I first
dramatically noticed my deficit in the area of
physical affection. By nature, I love hugs. I desperately wanted to be at the receiving end of a
loving hug.

Any hug felt *so* good! Who the giver was didn't
matter. If it was a caring man, I was overwhelmed
with warm, fuzzy shock waves, especially if he
was wearing a make-me-melt cologne.

I needed to discern a healthy balance. I realized
that such physical contact, although brief and
temporary, met a need. I made sure I got and gave
a generous quota of hugs each week. Whenever
opportunities arose, I shamelessly took advantage
of them, though church was the most frequent
place. And you know what? I *still* need hugs and
probably always will, even though the intensity of
the need has diminished.

Yet in order to keep these hugs healthy, I had to
guard my emotional and physical responses with
certain people (namely, attractive married men).

The hugs were nice. I did not want to begin fantasizing, to wait for the next one or to want more.

Another life-saving routine I have incorporated is full-body massage from a licensed massage therapist. One hour every month! At first I considered this a luxury, but now definitely a necessity. Not only is it extremely pleasurable, but it has documented physical and emotional health benefits. Because many people view this as a luxury, I don't broadcast it (until now).

Accountability is a big word for a simple safeguarding process: Choose a trustworthy, supportive person to confide in. Be honest about your vulnerability, and request that they be bold in checking in with you to help you stay on track. Offer to help keep them accountable in an area with which they struggle.

One thing I'm learning to remember is that *nothing feels as good as being right with God.*

We as humans have been designed by God to require touch. I strongly encourage you to examine your options and take care of yourself in this frequently overlooked area.

Reflection:

1. Write out a statement of your value: I am a valuable person because _____.
   Include the ultimate basis for your worth, and then list as many of your character strengths as you can. (Ask a friend for help if you get stuck.)

2. Name one to three areas you want to improve in your appearance; name one to three unchangeable areas you want to learn to accept; name one to three positive features you can really enjoy.

3. Is there something you're accusing yourself of that perhaps is not true? What areas honestly need work?

4. When are your feelings of loneliness most intense? After acknowledging the pain, what positive methods can you use to prepare for those times? What beneficial things fill the void?

5. What choices are you making to stay sexually pure?

Chapter 3

Him: Your Ex-Husband

Saturday, the 9th

What a day! Ugh!

Danny has been awful!!

Steve's a @#!&%*!!

And I'm beat. I feel like I've been running on "reserve" tank for weeks—perhaps I'm on "fumes" now.

"We have this treasure in jars of clay to show that this all-surpassing power is from God and not from us" (2 Corinthians 4:7).

My jar of clay is shot. Only God can keep me going emotionally and physically at this point.

Monday, the 26th

Cried last night, not for me (for the first time), but for Steve. Honestly begged God's mercy and grace for him.

Please draw him back to You, and may he know You as never before.

"To have and to hold, from this time forth . . ." Well, at least until the divorce. This man to whom I committed my life, shared my body and soul and had his baby—who is he now? And how do I relate to him?

Of all the paradoxes in the universe, this one is the most mind-boggling and gut-wrenching. He's gone from being the most wonderful man on the face of the earth and to whom I willingly gave my life, to the other extreme of being this enemy/stranger who only causes me pain.

I now have to go through the mental and emotional process of separating myself from him, reclassifying him into a new category and determining the healthiest way to relate to him.

1. Why do I feel so awkward when I use his name or refer to him?

Remember when you were first married? It felt so strange yet so wonderful to introduce yourself as Mrs. _____. Using the words "my husband" and calling myself a "wife" were so unfamiliar, yet exciting. Gradually it became routine.

In a similar way, marriage identities now must be undone. Yet this time the proud feelings have been replaced by shame, sadness and anger. Is he my "former husband," "ex-husband," "Danny's daddy" or just plain "Steve" or "Steve Smith"? (Of course, there are many other names I've used which cannot be printed here. But saying them sure felt good at the time!)

"Former husband" sounds so businesslike and matter-of-fact. We're in a disposable society. This term implies there are more where he came from. No hard feelings.

"Ex-husband" sounds even less refined, though it is a more common term. It's often associated with a negative context. (Keep your eyes open for bumper stickers—notice any bitterness?)

A common shortcut is just "my ex." It almost portrays a callous playfulness, a flippant approach. This seems to be a term to use later, in a casual setting, after you've healed and your new identity is well established.

The term "Danny's daddy" tries to sidestep the obvious connection implied: How did he become Danny's daddy? Yet in a situation involving the child, this is the easiest to use.

It is still difficult for me to say his name without affecting any connecting nerves. But as time goes on, I am able to detach little by little and referring to him becomes less awkward.

Two factors help in this area. First, sometimes the situation itself will dictate the most comfortable way to refer to him. If they know him, just use his name. If it's someone who knows your child, he can be ____'s daddy. In a more formal or unfamiliar setting, former husband or ex-husband are acceptable.

Second, time lessens the awkwardness. The longer we are apart, the more distant he becomes. He will probably always remain in his own category, and I am becoming more comfortable accepting his change in identity as separate from me.

2. How do I deal with the wide range of intense feelings I have toward him?

Part of the healing/growing process is feeling. *Really* feeling. Facing the feelings, identifying them, accepting them and then choosing what to do with them. As time passes, the frequency and intensity of the emotions taper off as long as I handle them in a healthy way.

What a relief to know that it is common and normal one day to wish he would die and another day to wonder how I can live without him. A lot may depend on each individual situation, but the most typical feelings are anger, guilt, anguish, loneliness, hate, love, depression, jealousy, bitterness and rejection.

When I realized it was OK for me to have these feelings, that they were neither right nor wrong in themselves, it freed me to deal with them as they surfaced. The best way for me was to consciously acknowledge the feeling, allow myself to feel it for as long as I needed, express it by talking, praying or writing and let it go.

The choice to let it go keeps the emotion from distorting perceptions of reality. If I were to dwell on the anger or on the lost love, either extreme would prevent me from healing.

In order to continue to process the painful feelings in a healthy way, I have had to learn to be

aware of signs that I'm holding in the feelings.
This is especially important at PMS time when
feelings can be so much more intense. Like a vol-
cano, each person will erupt in her own way if the
pressure has not been released through a good es-
cape valve (yelling, running, writing, crying, talking, swimming, praying, cleaning, pruning bushes,
singing, kicking, punching pillows). My unre-
leased anger shows up in my driving, and I've had
several near-accidents. Acid indigestion, snapping
at the kids, stress headaches, yelling at the dog or
binge eating are other signs that the feelings have
been buried rather than dealt with.

Feel the feelings, then deal with them, and
you'll be a step closer to healing.

*3. How long will I continue to dream about him, and
how do I process the feelings and contents of those
dreams?*

In attempting to make sense out of my dreams,
I start by remembering the source: me. Everything in that dream originated from my mind, in-
corporating a complex system of memories, hopes,
conscious and sub-conscious feelings. The value in
facing my dreams when I'm awake is in the discovering of submerged feelings. *My* feelings.

The types of dreams I've had about my ex-husband have covered a wide range of emotions and
were often reflective of the situation at the time.

One very vivid dream occurred in the heat of the
divorce proceedings. In my dream, my son Danny

and I were in the car and Steve was driving. It was dark, and we were on a winding mountain road. Suddenly, Steve stepped on the accelerator, deliberately driving us off the edge of the cliff. Thankfully, I woke up before we all died. But the intensity of the dream stunned me for days.

At that point, I could have chosen the quick and comfortable way out—to ignore it. Put it out of my mind. "It's only a dream." But I realized it came from deep inside me and was an indicator of some heavy-duty feelings.

Facing it head on at a conscious level wasn't as painful as I expected. And I didn't need a psychotherapist. What I realized was that I was very afraid of Steve, that he was destroying us (and himself) and I felt out of control.

It was so freeing to sort out the specific feelings. Once I allowed them to surface I could feel them, deal with them and begin to heal from them. Feel, deal, heal. It's a great formula, but you have to take the first step.

Sometimes it was enough to think through the dreams. Other times I felt I had to write. And sometimes I needed to talk about it. As long as there was an outlet, a way for me to process it, I was fine.

I've had intensely angry dreams. Those weren't too difficult to interpret. But I did have to find a healthy way to unload the anger (talking, writing, yelling, racquetball, running, etc.).

The most baffling to me have been the sexual dreams. A certain recurring theme was troubling

me: We would have sex, but something inside of
me was telling me it wasn't right. I would wake up
feeling a mixture of disgust, guilt, sadness and anger. Sorting through each feeling and discovering
why I was feeling that way was important.

A significant breakthrough finally occurred—
and this was one dream I had to talk about (to
privileged people only!). In this dream Steve ap-
proached me to have sex again, and for the first
time I told him "no." Yippee! I felt so good when I
woke up. And after that, these dreams significantly tapered off.

Dreams will come and go. But I'm learning to
discover what I can about the feelings involved,
and then to let them go. Then I am free to face reality.

4. How and where do I set new boundaries?

With a newly defined relationship where formerly husband and wife are no longer one flesh
but two separate individuals, there are implied
boundaries. The problem is that both of you will
assume the boundaries should be set at different
places. I had to learn that if I didn't set the
boundaries, he would continue to intrude into my
life where he was no longer welcome. This required me to think through and decide where he
was imposing and what I needed to do about it.

The first area I needed to protect was my
house, my physical space. Since my ex-husband
had lived here for several years before he left, he

felt at home when he came to pick up our son. At first, I didn't see any reason why he couldn't come in. Often he offered to fix something or help out in some way, and sometimes he just wanted something he had left there. But it got to the point where I felt uncomfortable about letting him in. I realized that although I liked it when he helped out, I was compromising.

I was just fooling myself because it felt like old times to have him around. But the old times were no more, and it was time for me to draw the line. I wanted my home to be mine, which meant he was no longer welcome to just come in like a family member. There was nothing wrong with being cordial, but that did not require allowing him into the house. Sometimes now I let him in, and he waits in the living room. But the decision is mine. Some people don't even let the ex-spouse in the house. That is a personal decision. For me, I had to accept the reality of the divorce and then decide where to draw the line. It was scary the first time I told him "no," but each time it has gotten easier.

A second area of consideration was setting verbal limits. The telephone calls from him were difficult for me. I had mixed feelings (and still do) when he called. I had to ask him not to call me at work unless it was an emergency. Now he leaves messages on my answering machine at home. When he calls me at home, as long as there is a good reason, it is fine. I am happy when he calls just to talk to Danny, and often we need to discuss visitation details. But those first few months, he called to unload. I realized it was not only OK but also very effective to tell him I didn't care to hear any more. Once I even hung up on him. Now that's a pretty clear boundary!

Some people are more verbally abusive than others. During our separation, my ex-husband became volatile, often bombarding me with abusive language. There were temper tantrums complete with rounds of uncensored ammunition, and there were the cutting cynical remarks.

Not being a fighter by nature, I was usually tongue-tied and defenseless. (I thought of wonderful responses hours later!) I had to learn to distinguish between the words that were worthy of a response and the words that required me to walk away. What helped was to detach my ego and try to remember the source—an angry, mixed-up person. Then I was free to choose how best to respond.

The third area in which I realized I needed to set boundaries was in my thinking, my mental space. I contrived a life-saving image which helped me survive the verbal assaults: Steve is a porcupine. Yes, a porcupine. (For one thing, it helped me get him down a few notches so I felt less intimidated.) I acknowledged the fact that his words pricked me. They hurt. But they weren't deadly, they didn't last and they could be removed. Visualizing him as a porcupine helped me disarm him in my mind. I imagined removing and discarding his verbal jabs. It still hurt, but I knew I would be OK.

So sometimes the boundaries need to be physical, sometimes they need to be verbal and sometimes they need to be mental.

5. Now that the divorce is final, how do I handle smaller item negotiations or discern manipulations without an attorney?

I am a person highly motivated to please others, and in the past I did almost anything to avoid conflict. It has taken me a while to build the confidence in myself that is necessary for healthy negotiating, whether it's a general visitation schedule or something specific.

The day he left, I amiably helped him pack some things, such as towels and dishes. (I did make a point to give him the garage-sale-quality items.) But it was either co-dependence or naiveté on my part to actually assist him in this devastating departure. ("He just needs some time alone to think. Right. Wake up, Welby!")

Every so often he came back for something, and until the common property was legally divided, I didn't have much say. Thankfully, he wasn't unreasonable in his requests.

As time passed and reality set in, I began understanding the need for boundaries in the area of material possessions. In order to protect what I had, I had to internally give myself both permission and power to stand firm.

The scriptural principles of loving your enemies, giving your brother your coat and turning the other cheek, weighed heavily on me (Luke 6:27-36). How was I to respond in a Christlike way, yet take responsibility for my own needs?

One verse says, "If the unbeliever leaves, let him do so" (1 Corinthians 7:15). The Lord did not intend for us to subsidize sinners and give in to their every demand. The underlying principles are love, compassion and forgiveness. God also tells us that our primary responsibility is our family (1 Timothy 5:8). Steve had chosen to remove himself from the family, and therefore I am no longer responsible to give him everything he wants.

I *am* accountable for my attitude and actions, which does not imply giving in to unreasonable demands. Learning to say "no" or having the confidence to negotiate with a level head has been a process. Each time it gets easier.

But my conscience is clear because I am seeking to honor God in my motives. When I have been tempted to withhold from him out of spite, vengeance or power, the situation only gets worse. There is no satisfaction in the long run from returning hurt for hurt. I have had to accept the fact that there are no winners in a divorce, and it will never be fair. Letting go of that has been difficult, but freeing.

The biggest step of growth in learning to stand firm was when Steve wanted to borrow the video camera after the property division had already occurred. One of the first things I learned was not to make instant decisions under pressure. "Let me give that some thought, and I'll let you know tomorrow." Even if I'm fairly certain of my answer, it allows me time to get input from friends, feel confident about the decision and then find the most effective way to word my response. Another thing I'm learning in negotiating is to try to accompany a "no" answer with one or two alternatives. This helps me not be the "bad guy" but puts the choice back on him.

Well, I'm glad I took the time to prepare, or I would have been toppled by his explosive reaction regarding the video camera. I had to find the root issue and identify the underlying principle of this conflict. The issue here was *not* the video camera. It was the issue of *boundaries*: The line had been drawn, and my possessions were no longer at his disposal. Remaining firm on the issue gave me an opportunity to say "no" to him and survive.

I spoke calmly but firmly. I had purposed to detach my emotions from the situation and to remember that I am not obligated to provide reasons for my decision. I said, "I do not feel comfortable letting you or anyone else borrow this. I would be happy to come along to the event and tape it myself if my schedule permits." Period. After observing a few amusing attempts to manipulate me into changing my mind, I continued to stand firm. I kept repeating the same thing in the same tone of voice.

He exploded like a strong-willed, two-year-old boy having a tantrum in a 200-pound body. And I survived. I was OK.

Since that day, he knows I will stand firm. He'll still try to persuade me from time to time, usually around Christmas and Danny's birthday, about some monetary concern or about wanting more visitation time.

But I'm OK because I am no longer dependent on his approval for my sense of well-being. I am free to make decisions the healthy way, to state them clearly and then to stand firm.

6. What do I wear when he comes to get the kids?

Once you've lived with a man for years, who has seen you naked, at your best and at your worst, does it really matter how you are dressed when he's not coming to see you anyway? I wrestled with this time and time again.

And why when I saw his car pull up was I driven to run to the bathroom mirror to brush my hair or put on lipstick?

In dealing with this issue, I discovered two underlying approaches. One way I viewed him as a nonperson, putting a wall of denial between us to shield myself from the pain of who he really was. The other way I acted as though his feelings and thoughts were of utmost importance. The first view might seem logical: Since he has seen me naked for years, then it really doesn't matter. I could answer the door in my pajamas, braless in a T-shirt or in a towel if I had just stepped out of the shower. I could have bad breath and hairy legs—what would it matter? Why waste energy on this person who really doesn't exist?

Then at the other extreme is the manipulative approach. I could purposely dress a certain way in order to evoke a response on his part, whether or not he verbalizes it. There have been many times when I've wanted to make him regret his decision to leave. One option here would be to dress in a sexy way to frustrate him and make him realize what he's missing. Another idea is to impress him with the successful, corporate career look I "just happen" to be wearing, with hair and makeup to perfection.

The first time I played the game it was kind of fun. Not too long after Steve had first left and he was coming to get Danny, I was getting ready to go out and had my black slip peeking seductively out from under my robe. He was definitely curious and tried to get me to tell him where I was going. I raised my eyebrows as if to say, "Wouldn't you like to know, and don't you wish it were with you?" I never did tell him. That would have been anti-climactic and counter-productive and, of course, no fun for me. (Our church music group was singing that evening.)

After that night, I realized I didn't want to play games with him. For me, neither the seemingly logical nor the manipulative approach was a healthy alternative. To be honest, I've tried both, with no results from him and a pile of emptiness for me. After accepting that I am OK apart from him and releasing the desire for vengeance (a repeat process), I have no need for manipulation. Because of my self-respect and my newfound separateness from him, I found it best when I treated him as I would any other person.

So I have sought a balance where I am still free from seeking a response from him, yet I maintain my modesty and self-respect. I make sure I am decent, presentable enough to be able to greet even our pastor if he dropped by unexpectedly. Yet I do not go out of my way to look good even if I know Steve may criticize me. It has been a process, and I still have to consciously tell myself I do not have to do a final check in the mirror. His arrival and his opinion (if he even cares) do not change the fact that I am *OK*.

7. Why is it so difficult to pray for him, and should I if I don't want to? What do I pray?

For a long time I could not pray for my ex-husband. I thought that praying was something I *should* be doing, but there was a huge brick wall in front of me that I couldn't get past. I didn't have any desire to pray.

It was OK for me not to pray for him at that point. If I had tried, I would have felt like a hypocrite. Someone pointed out to me that there were others who were praying for him. Steve *was* being prayed for.

Other times when I did feel like praying, my prayers came under the theological classification of imprecatory prayers such as David invoked on his enemies in Psalms. For example, Psalm 35:8 says, "Let destruction come upon him unexpectedly, and let his net that he has hidden catch himself; into that very destruction let him fall" (NKJV). I'm sure Steve would be grateful that God chose not to answer those prayers.

Gradually, the vindictive passion within me subsided, and I became apathetic again. From a purely human perspective, I could not muster any love or compassion for him.

After a period of time when I continued to seek the Lord and to make godly choices, the brick wall started to crumble. A genuine burden for him, small as it was, came indirectly as a result of my concern for my son, and ultimately from a desire to glorify God in every area of my life. For the first time I was able to pray for him. I began to pray that Steve give his whole heart back to the Lord for Danny's sake. The more time he spent with his dad, the more I realized how desperately Danny needed the influence of a godly man in his life. So my heartfelt prayer has been (and will continue to be) that Steve walks with the Lord, immerses himself in the Word and is a positive, godly influence in Danny's life.

If there were no child involved, I could still pray for Steve now. This is by the grace of God who put that willingness in me. My desire is for God to be glorified, however He chooses, through Steve. God may speak softly to Steve, or He may speak through some form of tragedy. I don't presume to tell God how to do His business.

After making the choice to be *willing* to pray
that God's will be done, I now can sometimes
even feel the passion as I pray. At other times I
pray just because it's the right thing to do. Either
way, my prayer is that God would be glorified,
first through me, and then through Steve and
Danny.

James 5:16 tells us to "pray for each other so
that you may be healed." I like to think of this as
having a dual application, as I pray that Steve
would be healed, then in that process I myself can
also heal.

Reflection:

1. Practice saying your ex-husband's name out
   loud (nicely), and then in sentences as if you
   were introducing him (nicely) to a co-worker.

2. On a separate sheet of paper, record your feelings toward your ex-husband every day for a
   week. Write out as much as you need to. Then
   destroy the paper (cut it, burn it, rip it, flush
   it).

3. Describe your most recent dream about him,
   not only what happened, but what *you did* and
   what *you felt*. What are those feelings telling
   you?

4. In what area(s) do you feel your ex-husband is
   intruding uninvited? What steps can you take
   to draw a healthy boundary line?

5. Think of a situation (real or potential) where your ex-husband makes an unreasonable request or demand. Practice your response out loud.

6. What clothing have you determined to be acceptable and unacceptable to wear when you see your ex-husband? What is the primary factor motivating your decision?

7. Where are you in the process of being able to pray for him? If you are praying, what do you pray? If not, can you ask someone else to pray for him?

Chapter 4

Daily Life: Going On

Tuesday, the 12th

I have plenty to do and am enjoying my life, rather than sitting around feeling sorry that I don't have a husband.

Adjusting to the reality of my divorce, accepting my new identity, clarifying the new unnatural relationship with my ex-husband . . . each is a process which will take time. Meanwhile I still have to get up in the morning, face the day and carry out the responsibilities of life. Sometimes just waking up can be the most unbearable task: The piercing pain in my gut is engulfed by the crushing load of all I have to do.

Training myself to look up to the Lord the first thing each morning has been a real encouragement. Whatever I'm facing in the day ahead, I commit it to Him and pray that I keep my eyes on Him *whatever* happens. I know God is in charge of my day.

I try to remember to feel the feelings as they come and that I can make choices. I remind myself that my job right now is to survive, and it is OK to do whatever is necessary to take care of myself. And it feels so good to remember that God loves me far greater than any other person loves me, even myself.

1. How can I best be prepared to accept the reality of the divorce?

Sometimes it's the little things that throw us for a loop. For instance, filling out forms is part of living in America, and marital status is frequently near the top.

The first time I had to indicate in writing that I was *DIVORCED* was in the doctor's office. I felt like I was confessing to a crime, I was a failure and I was a second-class citizen. My writing hand needed an extra push. And, of course, I just knew everybody was staring.

Another seemingly insignificant hurdle was actually saying the "D" word (divorce). It wasn't so bad when I was talking with people who knew me and had known the situation all along. But I really tripped up when speaking to people who either didn't know me or hadn't even known we were separated. To say the least, it was awkward for everyone.

Psychologists use a process called desensitization when an individual needs to become anesthetized or more tolerant toward a certain stimulus. It works in a manner similar to building a callous. I wish I had practiced saying and writing the word divorce.

"I am divorced."
"We are no longer married."
"We are divorced."
"The divorce was final in July."

By saying it, not only does my tongue become more comfortable unloading the word, but my ears hear it, and my mind begins to believe it. And each time I do it with a little less pain and revulsion.

It is a fact. I do not have to explain or apologize. But it's only a matter of time before I must own it, and the sooner, the better.

2. Now that he is gone, what can I do to make this my home?

Since divorce settlements usually leave at least one party worse off financially, selling the house is often necessary. Some women take advantage of this opportunity to move and made a fresh start. They want to make it easier to avoid the painful memories and establish a new identity.

Others choose to stay in the house or apartment, as was the case for me. I was the one who had discovered this house and had fallen in love with it. Also, I wanted to stay where Danny could feel secure and close to his friends.

If you choose to stay, some modifications will be in order. One woman went out immediately and spent $15,000 remodeling her bedroom. For her, that did wonders. (The only thing that would have done for me was put me $15,000 in debt.) For most of us, we need to seek affordable, creative alternatives.

The space that was his (closets, workbench, favorite reading chair, desk, bookshelf, dresser) needs to be claimed by you and replaced in a way that reflects who you are. These flagrant sources of potential pain can now be transformed to sources of pleasure.

Initially painful to face, the closet was a relatively easy place for me to begin. I just spread my stuff out and eventually filled the whole thing, dressers too. (I have no idea what I'll do if I ever remarry!)

Next, I updated the kitchen with new countertops and wallpaper. This was an opportunity to
release some bottled-up resentment, express who I
am and give myself a much-needed treat. For
years I had lived with a kitchen decorated in or-
ange-and-green print wallpaper and school-bus
yellow countertops. I had always hoped to have a
memorial service for the old decor and bring to
life a room that was pleasing to me. So I counted
the cost and treated myself with a delightful "new
kitchen."

Rearranging the bedroom was also a top priority, as it will be with every newly divorced
woman. I was driven to make it feel like an entirely different room. Rearranging everything and
hanging some new pictures made a significant difference.

Being a sucker for new towels and bedspreads, I
seized this opportunity with great enthusiasm. I
lusted after so many beautiful bed coverings, but I
fell in love with one in particular. It was me! And it
perfectly matched the carpet and paint. But it was
so feminine. Here I switched from right brain (feeling) to left brain (calculating). What if I get remarried? No normal man would want this decor. Then
I realized: I can choose what I like. I gave myself
permission to enjoy my new life and my newfound
freedom of expressing myself in my home.

Do not put your life on hold, passing up opportunities for right now just because of the "what
ifs." Be wise, yes, but do what you can to enjoy
the reasonable pleasures of today.

There have been other gradual changes, such as rearranging furniture, painting here and there, buying new plants. It was fun to transform his study into a play and exercise room. Now it takes a conscious effort to remember it as it was.

In claiming the home which you previously shared with your mate as now entirely your own, you begin to bury the daily reminders and, in essence, make a statement about your newly embraced identity. You also give yourself permission to enjoy your home.

3. Why is the house suddenly so much scarier at night? Do I have to live with constant fear?

I don't know about you, but when I'm alone, my house seems to creak and groan, convincing me that there are people walking around. Funny how I never noticed these noises while Steve was here.

Whether or not our ex-husbands could have successfully fended off an intruder is irrelevant now. The point is we need to be safe and to feel safe. The actual steps required to accomplish this will vary with each individual and her situation.

Although it would be nice if a friend or relative could safeguard your home at no charge, necessary upgrades will likely be costly. But when you weigh the benefits, this is the best investment you'll ever make. You'll sleep at night, you'll know your children are safe, and you can come home to a secure house.

There were three things I needed to do to be and to feel safe. Only one was relatively expensive. And all three have been well worth it.

First, I got a good watchdog. Our other (non-watchdog) dog had just died, so the timing worked well. It's not easy to find a ferocious watchdog that is good with kids. But keep looking. If anybody comes near my house, my dog lets them know she means business. And I sleep very well at night. (The small price I pay is dog food and being the pooper scooper.)

Second, I needed a phone by my bed with a lighted dial in case of emergency. That was easy.

Third, I had bars installed on my basement windows and a security door added to the back door. These things did cost some money, but even if I never get would-be intruders, my peace of mind is well worth it.

Although I didn't feel it was necessary in my situation, some women will have the locks changed since the ex-husband probably still has a key.

Other ideas to consider might be a secure fence, an alarm system, outdoor lights and a most controversial item—a gun. (I don't have one and have mixed feelings about the issue. Seek counsel and do what *you* need to do.)

It's wonderful to know the Lord promises to protect us and give us peace. (See Appendix C.) But He also gives us wisdom to take the practical steps we can to reduce the risk of danger.

*4. Now that I'm on my own, how can I be tough enough
to survive, yet preserve a tender, beautiful spirit?*

If you had to choose between having the reputation of a tough, crusty old lady or a wilted little doormat, which would it be? Contrary to
what many of us have been led to believe, it
doesn't have to be either. Our ideal role model,
Jesus, exemplifies love, tenderness and humility
as well as strength, decisiveness and righteous
anger.

We are encouraged as godly women to have the
inner beauty of a gentle spirit. (See 1 Peter 3:3-4.)
This is an underlying attitude which should be at
the heart of all we do.

What does a gentle spirit mean and what does it
not mean? For starters, it does *not* mean you have
to be a wimpy pushover and let people take advantage of you as you smile sweetly. It does *not* mean
you must wait for people to come to you and offer
help. It does *not* mean you can never risk offending anyone. It does *not* mean you are robbed of the
right to ask that your needs be met.

It *does* mean that as you exercise your right to
take care of your needs, you can do so confidently
with a beautiful, gentle spirit. For example, you
can talk to customer service in a quiet but firm
voice and continue to restate your complaint as
often as necessary without ever becoming emotional. It is often helpful to offer some alternative
solutions. You can tell the telephone solicitor,
"We're not interested, thank you," and repeat it

firmly as she continues to argue. You may even have to hang up. And that's OK.

Assertiveness was a controversial buzzword of the '80s, supposedly being the middle ground between passive and aggressive. *The Merriam Webster Dictionary* defines assert as "to state positively, to maintain against opposition." Some synonyms are "declare," "affirm" and "claim." Assertiveness is a healthy way of communicating what I need, either proactively or in defense. When carried out with a kind attitude at the core, assertiveness is the tool that enables gentleness and strength to work hand in hand.

Recently I chose to approach my boss for a much-needed raise. It was one of the scariest things I've ever done. I could have gone to him kicking and screaming—or crying—over the unfairness of my pay rate, equipped to tell him where he could go if he turned me down. Or, at the other extreme, I could have crawled to him apologetically to put in my request, fully expecting to be patted on the head or kicked out of the office.

What I had to do was rehearse with my friends a very matter-of-fact statement. True assertiveness does not accuse or attack. It states the facts and how I feel about the situation. It is a confident invitation to join together in solving a mutual problem.

I was able to say clearly what I needed to say without backing him into a corner. It depleted my adrenalin supply and left me shaking for an hour afterward, but *I did it!* He thanked me for coming to him, and three conversations later, we arrived at a solution.

Whether it's just saying no to a phone solicitor, sending a friend home when you're tired or asking a neighbor for help—you are free to communicate your need while at the same time displaying the beauty of a godly woman.

Strong, but not overpowering. Gentle, but not weak. Now that's a healthy balance.

5. What's the best way for me to deal with the change in family meals and my lack of motivation for cooking nice meals?

Each woman has different feelings about her place in the kitchen. I have always been partial to the old-fashioned scenario so memorably modeled on "Father Knows Best" and "Leave It to Beaver." The husband goes to work each day and the wife takes care of the domestics, primarily mothering, cooking and cleaning.

Before circumstances dictated that I go back to work, I *loved* my role as stay-at-home wife and mother. Cooking was enjoyable because I was home and I had time.

Now the scenario has shifted. Mornings are consumed by getting Danny and myself dressed and out the door on time. So much for a breakfast of oatmeal, eggs and homemade muffins. Try a banana and a piece of toast. Or cold cereal and milk.

Lunches are packed with just the basics.

By the time we get home, cooking is the last thing I want to do. Besides, I'm usually so hungry I'd have it all eaten before it was cooked anyway. So we usually settle for sandwiches, pizza, salads, a cooked vegetable, cereal or leftovers. A friend of mine cooks up big batches of soup, freezes them in meal-sized portions and pops them into the microwave.

Besides just being energy-depleted come dinnertime, I also struggle with apathy. Why expend a lot of effort to make a great meal when there's no one to appreciate it? Not that Steve always raved about a good meal, but at least the fact that we sat down for dinner was itself motivating.

Three things may help you with this issue. First, remember you are in a survival mode right now. Your goal each day is to take care of your needs and those of your family. Attempting to be Betty Crocker is not realistic. Shake off the "shoulds" and release yourself from any self-imposed or society-imposed guilt. If you're buying nutrient-rich food (fruits, vegetables, whole grains) and serving well-balanced meals, who cares how fancy they are?

Forget the canning, the marinades, the time-consuming gourmet preparations. Eat a bagel for dinner if you want. The nutritional content is identical to cooked pasta, and all you have to do is open the bag and take a bite. How about carrot sticks or an orange instead of a fancy vegetable dish? A salad or already chopped-up stir-fry? The possibilities are limitless for simple, quick, healthy meals.

Second, consider taking advantage of Saturday mornings or certain special occasions. These present wonderful opportunities to establish traditions (pancake breakfast on Sunday mornings, split pea soup on Halloween, special meals for birthdays). When you know you will have time to cook and time together, you can do more.

Third, it's important to spend some time each day with your children. Food is the natural magnetic force. Danny and I always have our "last snack" together in the kitchen (TV is off). It gives us a time to talk, laugh and make memories. (And I don't even have to cook!)

6. Should I feel guilty about actually enjoying some of the side benefits of one less husband?

Indulge yourself for a moment. Think of all the things you are secretly glad about now that your ex-husband is gone. Can you whip out a list of five things? Or is there some shadowy cloud forbidding you to think like that?

It took me a long time to be able to enjoy the positive without feeling guilty. I needed to face the dissonance head-on by sorting through my thoughts and feelings.

After digging deeply, I was surprised to discover that at the heart of my problem were two basic fears. First, I was afraid that allowing myself to enjoy any part of this divorce aftermath would betray my grief. Like a widow in black, I was grieving the death of my marriage. It wouldn't be proper to allow myself to be happy about anything directly related to his being gone. Maybe in time as the cloud was lifted I would be able to find some benefits, I thought.

A second fear was that acknowledging any form of happiness resulting from his departure might be an admission of a hidden desire all along to be rid of him.

In response to these two fears, I needed to give myself permission to grieve as long as I needed, realizing that there would be increasingly larger spots of cheer as the healing progressed. Enjoying those moments of relief—and even feeling happy—is good, is allowed and is necessary.

I also had to examine my conscience again, clearing myself from the false accusations of wanting him gone. With my heart open before the Lord, I knew that while I hadn't been a perfect wife, I loved Steve and wanted our marriage to work.

After I had done the necessary soul-searching, I had a choice: to shrink under the cloud, stifling any potential relief or joy *or* to thrive, welcoming any positive feelings that came.

Here are some of the things I *don't* miss a bit. You may want to add a few of your own to the list:

- picking up after him
- his early rising or coming to bed late
- putting the toilet seat down

- wondering what latest gadget of his
  would appear on the credit card bill
- extra laundry and ironing
- bothering with birth control
- snoring (and other nightly disturbances).

And on the positive side, I enjoy these things:

- lighter grocery budget
- more room in the closet
- less meal preparation
- fewer dishes to do
- more time to myself in the bathroom
- eating what and when I want
- freedom!

Reflection:

1. Practice writing and saying, "I am divorced," (or a similar statement using the "D" word).

2. Starting with the room that has the most memories of "him," decide how you can affordably reclaim your home and make it yours.

3. Do you feel safe in your home? If not, what can you do?

4. In what area(s) do you need to be assertive? Practice what you will say.

5. Keeping in mind that you are in a survival mode these days, make a seven-day menu of easy-to-prepare, nutritious meals. What can you add occasionally just for fun (fortune cookies, a seasonal centerpiece, colorful paper plates, etc.)?

6. Dare to list five things you actually enjoy about your ex-husband's absence.

Chapter 5

Her: The Other Woman

Friday, the 2nd

Had a real hard night—kept waking up thinking about HER. How could he? How can he do all the things with her he's always done only with me?

I need to realize in this world we will have trouble—but cheer up—He has overcome the world!!

Thursday, the 11th

I had to face her—I was compelled to confront reality. . . .

What a thing to say—Why am I so nice and so loving to that @%#* and his #*@%?!

*T*en years ago, if you had asked me which of us would be more likely to have an affair, I would have said me. In my mind, Steve was the last person in the world who would take off with another woman.

Before our divorce, I sometimes had nightmares in which he was with someone else. These were painfully disturbing. But it didn't take long to reassure myself that it would never really happen; after all, it was just a dream. In actuality, my dreams turned out to be a dreadful sneak preview.

Every situation is different. Some ex-husbands may never have another woman, although that is rare. Some leave their wives for a homosexual relationship. Others may have a string of women. In my case, he had his eye on her for about a year before he actually made any move toward her.

Whatever your circumstances, chances are high that you will eventually have to deal with "another woman."

1. What is the healthiest way to process my feelings after the initial shock of finding out about "her"?

It is common to experience a wide range of emotions cropping up at any moment, from feeling cheated and abused to feeling self-righteous and vindictive. If it's an ugly feeling, you name it, you got it. You may wake up plagued with guilt, wondering what you did wrong, and go to bed

consumed with overwhelming rage, bent on retaliation. Each of us will have a different response
and progress through a variety of feelings at a different rate.

I can vividly recall the morning I found out
about Susan. Up until then, all I had were uncon-
firmed suspicions. I was home alone and had just
received a phone call from a businessman in town
who happened to mention seeing them together.
During the course of the conversation, the nature
of my husband's relationship with this woman became undeniable.

My immediate reaction, sort of a survival
mechanism, was to blank out. I was so stunned I
went numb. Then I switched to denial: There
must be some mistake.

In the process of making my way to my bedroom, reality set in. I fell to the floor, curled up in
a fetal position and wailed. In all my life I had
never cried like this. Every ounce of my body
shook intensely, as if to rid itself of this unbearable deluge of feelings so deep they were unidenti-
fiable.

That moment was the beginning of a long road
of healing.

The rest of the day was a blur. But without a
doubt I spent it crying and talking to my mom
and closest friend. I don't think I had the strength
to do much more.

As the initial shock gradually became more
bearable, I was able to write in my journal, identify the feelings, feel the feelings, talk to my coun-

selor and supporters, pray, read the Bible and cling to God's promises.

Had I remained in a state of denial or repressed those nuclear-powered feelings, I would not be where I am today. By the grace of God and the love of those surrounding me, I faced the pain and walked through the valley.

2. What do I say at our inevitable first face-to-face encounter?

There was a bit of irony in the entire progression of events that culminated in Steve's affair. He had met Susan at work and had become a "counselor in shining armor," listening to her relational woes. It had never occurred to me not to trust him in prior counseling situations, and in fact, I admired him for his desire to help others.

Several months passed and she finally accepted his invitation to church. Like the friendly, hospitable person I am, I warmly welcomed her (and her boyfriend) and saved seats so we could all sit together. Sweet, wasn't it?

Until the next day when he told me he didn't want to be married anymore. Three weeks later he moved out. And it wasn't long before they began their relationship.

A few weeks after that he brought her with him to my house to pick up Danny. That was the memorable moment of our inevitable first face-to-face encounter.

As I peered out the kitchen window and saw

her sitting in his car at the bottom of the driveway, my body instantly generated 10,000 volts of
electricity, super-charging my heart, my mind and
my blood pressure (not to mention the gallon of
battery acid dumped into my stomach).

The intensity of the feelings managed to short-
circuit my logic, and as if driven by an unseen
force, I marched out the door, past Steve and
down the driveway. He did an about-face, following me in an attempt to prevent World War III.

Everybody I had talked with knew about Steve
and Susan—my mom, my friends, my support
group at church—and all had been faithfully praying about the whole situation. In our less spiritual
moments, there had been bitterness, anger and de-
grading remarks.

I had fantasized about some very clever, cutting
and cruel comments I could make to her and felt
very justified in my right to do so. I had wished
that she would get zits and get fat. I had hoped her
ex-boyfriend would kill them both. I would lie at
night in pain and cry myself to sleep.

The only way I survived was to let the feelings
come (ouch!) and to fill my heart with God's
Word. Writing down my hatred and hopelessness,
crying, beating the pillow on the bed, talking to
my friends and counselor, walking, running, telling my feelings to the Lord, yelling—all helped
process the poisonous feelings so I could be
cleansed from them.

And when we empty ourselves of the bad, we
need to refill with something good. For me, that

something good was Scripture. God's promises warmed me with comfort like a hug from Mom, a soft cozy blanket and a bowl of soup when you don't feel good.

Making healthy choices enabled me to survive. But when the moment of our meeting came, all my forethought and fantasy did not prepare me. As good as it would have felt to "let her have it" both physically and verbally, there would have been unpleasant repercussions beginning immediately and continuing indefinitely. Had my brain been fully functioning at the time, I could have figured out that angry confrontation would only add fuel to an already devastating and out-of-control fire.

And it would not bring Steve back.

I wish I could say I have the perfect solution. I don't. Since every situation is unique, seek wisdom and self-control from your supernatural Source, the Lord. He will give you the right words at the right time.

That is the only explanation I have for what came out of my mouth the moment I stood face to face with Susan.

As I marched down the driveway, propelled by a ravaging vengeance, I had no clue what I would do or say. I just knew I had to see her with my own eyes, and I had to take advantage of this opportunity to hurt her.

I boldly opened the car door, had the presence of mind to shoot up a quick prayer for wisdom, and said, "Hi."

She smiled back (probably trembling as much as I was) and said, "Hi."

Then out of my mouth came the words, "I just want you to know there are a lot of people praying for you both." I shut the door and went back inside.

Do you think I ever would have planned that? But it was probably the most powerful, yet diffusing thing I could have said.

You're welcome to try it. Let me know how it goes.

3. How can I be sure I come out the winner when I compare myself to her?

A quick answer to that question is, you can't. Whenever you compare yourself with anyone, nobody comes out a winner. Competing with somebody inferior to myself (from my perspective) results in pride—no winners. Competing with somebody superior to me (from my perspective) results in discouragement—no winners again.

Unfortunately, in my pain I was not always making the healthiest choices. My self-esteem was shattered, and I just needed to feel good about myself. So I took a shortcut, or so I thought.

As females, it seems there is a basic survival instinct that leans toward competition with other females. Toss in a sin nature and add a man, then—look out! (Tune in to any daytime TV talk show and you're likely to see two women cat-fighting over a man.)

I'd like to think that I, an intelligent, cultured woman, would respond in a mature, rational manner to such a situation.

Oops.

The first question that immediately plagues the one who has been left behind is "What does *she* have that I don't?" And our initial impulse is to go through the necessary mental exercises to get the answer. At least, I did.

See my rational, mature conclusions?

> She's thinner.
> She's cuter.
> Her haircut is better.
> Her butt is smaller.

This, of course, only added to my depression. So in my logical, cultured mind-set, I did what any woman would do: I came up with what *I* have that *she* doesn't. My chest is bigger! And immediately I felt better.

But before long, I realized I had to go back to the beginning and take the full journey of healthy self-esteem. No shortcuts. I had to look at me, and me alone, not in comparison with anyone.

What are my strengths? What are my weaknesses? What are my beautiful qualities, both inner and outer? What do I need to change from *God's* perspective, and what do I need to learn to accept?

The Serenity Prayer provides a good balance:

"God, grant me the serenity to accept the things I cannot change, the courage to change the things I can, and the wisdom to know the difference."

Talking to my friends encouraged me, freeing me from a distorted view of myself and validating my positive attributes.

The irony of this whole comparison game is that all of the conclusions I drew had nothing to do with why he dumped me for her.

Reminding myself not to get sucked into the comparison trap has been an ongoing process. I am rebuilding my self-esteem on the solid fact that *God* loves me and has made me in *His* image.

No matter how thin, how young, how flawless her complexion, how good she is in bed . . . nothing can change who you are and how valuable you are to the Creator of the universe. Keep reminding yourself, and it will start to sink in.

Now *that* feels good.

4. How do I quickly process my reactive feelings when I see someone who looks like her or her children?

The poor kid didn't have a chance with me. As far as I was concerned, this innocent little boy in Danny's class looked too much like Susan's son for me to ever accept him. Consciously, I knew it was ridiculous. But subconsciously, the animosity was very real.

I've seen women at church or in the store who resemble her, and I have to catch myself before I act on the impulse to punch out their lights.

It's times like these when I'm thankful that my left brain is capable of overpowering my right brain. Logic can triumph over feeling.

But what do I do with the feelings that have been aroused, even though it was a false alarm?

Over and over again I have to remind myself to feel the feelings and process them in a healthy way. I have to acknowledge the anger and bitterness and pain. Then I have to get it out by talking, crying, writing, praying or running. One day I even set up some pillows, semi-dressed to resemble Susan. It felt so good to punch "her." (She was quite deformed when I was through with her.) Finally my anger turned to laughter.

Each woman has her own best way of dealing with the feelings. Just be sure not to downplay or ignore them. Feel, deal and heal.

By the way, I finally made myself give that little boy a hug. It felt good. Another step in the right direction.

5. What is the proper demeanor for additional contacts with her?

My relationship (if you can call it that) with Susan will never be normal. Humanly speaking, it will always feel, at best, like "What's wrong with this picture?" She has been a main character in the desolation of my life as I knew it. How am I supposed to communicate with her and relate to her in those painful and awkward moments when our paths must cross?

I guess we could claim this as a wonderful opportunity to apply the principles of feeling the feelings and making healthy choices. But first, let's brainstorm some options.

- Be mean and nasty; let loose with those choice words you've been storing up.
- Be sugary sweet and kill her with kindness.
- Be businesslike and formally cordial.
- Act like nothing happened and treat her like any other person.
- Ignore her if at all possible.

Although appealing and seemingly appropriate at times, I found that none of these options by itself is a healthy choice. After taking steps to be aware of my feelings and process them, there were other factors I needed to consider.

In deciding the best way for me to approach her, I had to take into account the details of the situation that day and determine what I wanted the results to be. For instance, most of my contacts with her were due to a visitation exchange. Because Danny would probably be present, I needed to consider what impact my behavior would have on him. Kids observe a lot more than we credit them for, and children of divorce are especially affected by the interaction of their parents.

As good as it would have felt to treat her as a bad person (some sinful, colorful words come to mind) or better yet, as a nonperson (not even worthy of bad words), it would not promote healing but would only make things worse.

At times like these, it's tough but crucial to remember our goal: Make healthy choices in order to survive and eventually heal.

Since my ex-husband eventually married the "other woman," I am thankful that I chose to relate to her in kindness. For me, there was a gradual progression, beginning with the necessary formal, businesslike attitude. We discussed only the essential details of the matter at hand. No wasted energy on extra smiles and cheery greetings.

Whenever I could avoid her, I did. I was not a glutton for punishment, and seeing her or talking to her just felt like a twist of the knife. But I did not do it in an obvious way out of retaliation. I set a boundary for my own survival.

As time passed and healing progressed, I think we both were able to let our guards down. It helped to remember through all this that I was just as much a threat to her as she was to me. She was probably wrestling with a hoard of her own feelings toward me and the whole situation.

We will never be best friends. And I will never be held responsible for her responses to me. My job is to treat her as Jesus would have, even if I never have the feelings to go with it.

6. Is it OK for me to refer to her as "what's-her-face"? (And don't tell me I have to pray for her.)

For the longest time, I had great difficulty getting her name out of my mouth gracefully. When talking about her, it was just easier to say "what's-her-face." And more fun.

Looking back, I see it as a playful way to deal with my lack of respect for her. It was a temporary, enabling, survival technique until I was capable of facing my deeper feelings toward her.

Simply put, I did not want to acknowledge her personhood or even her existence. To me, she was the most evil, villainous, heartless woman in the whole world. I considered it a gracious goal that I might some day come to tolerate her. But respect? Forgive? Like? Love? Ha ha ha! Nice joke.

Humanly speaking, the idea of loving her was laughable. But as a Christian, I couldn't ignore the words of the Lord: "Love your enemies, bless those who curse you, do good to those who hate you, and pray for those who spitefully use you and persecute you" (Matthew 5:44, NKJV).

"What does the LORD require of you? To act justly and to love mercy and to walk humbly with your God" (Micah 6:8).

The Scripture is rich with passages, such as First Corinthians 13 and Matthew 18:21-35, that emphasize love and forgiveness.

After all, when I realize the mercy that God has showered on me, how do I have any right to sit in judgment toward others? Yes, I have a right to feel my pain. I have a right to be angry. But vengeance is not my responsibility—that is the Lord's department. (See Deuteronomy 32:35.)

I am not responsible for punishing her. I am not responsible for her choices and her actions. I am not responsible for her responses to me. But I *am* responsible for my attitude, my actions and my reactions. Whether or not it ever makes any difference in *her* life, my choices will greatly impact *my* life. Bitterness, no matter how much I'm entitled to it, will only destroy me like cancer. It helps nobody and only hurts myself. Yes, I need to *feel* the feelings but not *feed* them.

There came a time when by choice I had to let go of my anger and be willing to forgive. The feelings behind the choice still have not come. I hope they will some day. It helps to remember that it is a process. Many times I've had to let go of the hatred and desire to retaliate and choose to love. And I will do so many times to come.

Am I better than Jesus? *He* loves her and offers His forgiveness. I pray to Him for the compassion and the grace to make healthy choices in my attitude toward her.

The choices become easier as time passes, and in the long run, I am the one who benefits. Galatians 6:7 reminds us that we reap what we sow. I want to reap a clear conscience, peace and healing.

Reflection:

1. If there was "another woman," describe your feelings when you found out. How have you processed those feelings (or do you still need to do so)?

2. Keeping in mind that your goal is healthy choices for *you*, what will you say to her when you see her?

3. If you've been comparing yourself to her, where has it gotten you? Practice writing and saying, "The God of the universe has created *me* (__your name__) and He loves me!"

4. What prompts your arousal of negative feelings toward her? What is the healthiest way(s) for you to deal with these feelings?

5. How do you treat her when you see or talk to her? Considering your goal of surviving and healing, would it be in your best interest to modify your approach? If so, how?

6. What does "forgive" mean to you? Where are you in the process of choosing to forgive her?

Chapter 6

Friends and Family: Defining New Roles

Monday, the 30th

Good to have Danny home tonight. It's so painful to think I'm sharing my son with another woman.

I hate her!

I hate him!

Danny spent the night with Steve at her place. Oh Lord, he's so innocent. Please protect him! Don't let him grow up thinking it's okay to act like this.

*D*ivorce changed my whole life, a major part of which is family and friends. The altered structure of my immediate family (that is, one less husband) has had an impact on everyone around me, particularly my parents, my former in-laws and my friends.

In the process of surviving these changes, I have had to apply the principles of making healthy choices in redefining my relationships with those around me.

1. How do I define my relationship with my parents now that I am single again?

Parents can be funny. Some never want their little girl to grow up, and others can hardly wait until she's eighteen and can move out. Wherever your parents may fit on the continuum, it's probably a good bet that in their minds you will always be their little girl.

That's been true for me. Going away to college was probably more traumatic for my mom than for me—and I cried myself to sleep every night for the first year.

My parents and I have always been close. I have been blessed with loving, God-fearing, generous parents who wanted only the best for me.

After college, marriage was my next major step in growing up and establishing my own identity. Motherhood was the third major step.

All of these stages of growth provided opportunities for good communication and a gradual transformation from a parent-child relationship to a friendship between adults (although a generation apart).

Unfortunately, the divorce severely disrupted the natural progression of my life and sent me running like a frightened child back into the safety of my parents' arms. Instinctively, both Mom and Dad were there to comfort, to advise and ready to beat the living daylights out of Steve.

I can never express how grateful I am for their love and support and godly words. Since they live in California, the phone company was also grateful. (We talked daily.)

But once again, I had some decisions to make. Dad wanted me to leave Oregon and move back "home" immediately. It would be like pretending none of this ever happened, going back in time to high school days.

As tempting as it was, I knew that would not be a healthy choice for me. I would be running away from my problems rather than facing them and resolving them.

It would have been a regression for me, discounting all the years and experiences that made me who I am as an adult. I needed to hold firmly to that maturity and use the pain of the divorce to *build* on that maturity, not as an excuse to go back to a dependent childlike relationship.

I will always love my parents and will always be their little "grown-up" girl. And I'm learning to embrace my childlike feelings as they come and go.

But I've grown up more since the divorce than any other time in my life, and I want to keep going forward. I am the one who has to define the parent-child relationship. I have to choose how emotionally dependent I should be on my parents. It's up to me to decide how much financial assistance to accept from them.

In keeping with the true nature of a caring parent, they want to offer advice. My mother has a knack for problem-solving and has always offered good advice (although it took me thirty-five years to appreciate it). In order to keep the lines of communication open, while avoiding unhealthy controlling and resentment, we made a deal which has worked well for us. I have asked her to share her thoughts and suggestions openly with me—I do want to hear them. Yet, she respects my right to decide whether or not to implement her ideas.

It may be necessary to set some boundaries or ground rules as you communicate your needs and desires with your parents.

There will be times when we need our parents more and times when healing results in our being able to give back to them.

Each woman needs to assess her situation and her relationship with her own parents. Maintain the bond you have with your parents and continue to build on it as you grow. Be open with them, and feel free to receive their love and compassion. But beware of getting sucked back into an unhealthy dependence.

2. What is my relationship with my former in-laws?

One word sums it up: awkward. As the details of each divorce vary, so will the feelings between former in-laws. There might be anger, bitterness, shame, sadness, confusion and maybe even denial.

I see two areas to consider in addressing former in-laws. First, how do I deal with my *feelings* toward them, and second, how does the divorce affect my *actions* toward them?

A lot will depend on the status of your relationship with them before the divorce. The closer you were, the harder you'll feel hit. Another factor will be their view of your ex-husband's innocence or guilt. Are they defensive of him and blaming you? Are they embarrassed by his actions and supportive of you? Are they trying to remain objective?

Whatever the situation, remember you are only responsible for *your* feelings and *your* actions. You want to make every attempt to process your feelings in a healthy way and make wise choices with your words and actions.

For me, it was more awkward and uncomfortable than it was painful. I felt like there were unwritten rules somewhere for how to act around them, but nobody told me what those rules were. I struggled with whether I should be transparent with my sadness and anger about Steve or if I should smile and portray a successful survivor attitude that says "I'm just fine."

I felt better when I remembered they were not feeling comfortable either.

Since they lived out of state, our contacts and phone conversations were infrequent. I discovered the best way for me to approach them was to be myself. When I got sidetracked by how I thought I *should* be, it only made things worse.

It was also helpful to remember that parents suffer from divorce, regardless of whose "fault" it is. I didn't want them to go through any more than they already had, and so in my stronger moments I tried to remain sensitive to them and downplay my role as a victim.

The healthiest approach for me was to be honest in a balanced way. For instance, I was truthful about my pain and struggles (to a certain degree) but was able to balance that out with comments of hope and going on. I didn't camp on the negative but shared some verse of hope or a specific lesson I was learning about God's faithfulness.

As far as actions, the biggest question I had was whether or not to continue initiating contact with them, particularly sending cards.

Was Steve the only reason for my relationship with them, and should I continue without him?

Again, that's a question that each person will have to decide. Where there is a mutual bond, the relationship often continues to grow without the former husband.

In my case, the decision was made easier because of Danny. Had there been no child in-

volved, our contacts would have probably de-
creased. But because Danny is their grandchild, I
have chosen to maintain the relationship. The
birthday, Christmas, Father's Day and Mother's
Day cards we send all come from him (with my
help, of course). As a facilitator of the grandpar-
ent-grandchild relationship, I continue to keep in
touch. They very much appreciate receiving photos as well as samples of his school work.

And it has turned out to be a nice two-way street.
I was brought to tears last week as Steve's mother
wrote a little note thanking me for being such a
good mother to Danny. That touched me deeply.

We do reap what we sow. It is up to each person to decide what the best choice is in relating
with former in-laws. In some cases, it may be necessary to cut things off, even if only temporarily.
In other cases, you may choose to be a responder
and not an initiator.

Whatever your choice, remember to relax and
be yourself. There is no right way to do this. As
you seek God's guidance and desire the best for
yourself and your family, you will be sowing
blessings to come.

*3. How do I maintain a healthy parent-child relation-
ship with my own children, meeting their needs and
avoiding becoming dependent on them to meet my needs?*

In the throes of the pain of my divorce, the last
thing I had energy for was parenting. There were
so many times when I felt like a needy child my-

self, and it was all I could do to survive, let alone care for my child. And that only added to my burden, because I knew Danny was going through his own trauma.

I really needed to lean on those around me, because I couldn't do it myself. I needed to talk and cry with my parents and friends. I needed to accept their offers to take Danny for short periods of time. I needed to feel free to ask for help. I needed to communicate with his teacher about the situation. And I needed extra sleep to be able to get up with Danny, since he woke up crying in the middle of every night.

Being aware of my own needs and weaknesses and finally accepting my inability to be supermom were my first steps toward a healthy relationship with Danny. Trying to live up to my expectations of perfect parenting only added feelings of guilt and anxiety.

The next step was to be sure his needs were met to the best of my ability.

- *Physical needs*: providing nutritious food, plenty of sleep, physical activity and play time, hugging and cuddling him and keeping one step ahead of outgrown shoes and clothes
- *Emotional needs*: telling him over and over how much I love him, assuring him I am here and am not leaving, reminding him how special he is, encouraging him to cry, teaching him healthy outlets for anger, laughing with him, hugging and cuddling with him

- *Social needs*: arranging time with his friends, putting on birthday parties (keeping things as simple as possible), encouraging team sports
- *Spiritual needs*: praying for him, praying with him, reading Bible stories to him, singing Christian songs with him, taking him to church, talking to him about the Lord and answering his questions

Many times I needed to borrow from other people to help meet Danny's needs. When I could, I read related books and articles addressing the fears and needs of children, particularly children of divorce. At one point I felt it necessary to take him to a professional Christian counselor. The wisdom, insight and support benefited both Danny and me. I also am grateful for a special friend that first year who planned and hosted his birthday party—I had no physical or emotional strength. All I did was show up. And I continued to ask people to pray for us both. Reaching out for help is OK; it is essential.

A third step for me was learning not to expect or allow Danny to fill the vacancy left by Steve. As humans it is natural for us to seek to satisfy the void in our life, and it is equally natural for our children to try to rescue us. They may be whiny and testy all day, but if you get injured or are down with a bad flu, they are usually right by your side. This response is partly a result of their insecurity in needing Mom to be a strong caregiver to them and partly because it makes them feel good to be able to help. We all like to be needed.

These natural tendencies become especially apparent in the aftermath of divorce. Yet it would not be a wise choice to yield to these unhealthy roles.

It was uncomfortable but helpful for me to be alert for this mind-set and accompanying actions. I caught myself many times expecting Danny to be an adult companion to me, rather than encouraging him to be the child he is. This involved consciously acknowledging my need, letting go of the expectation that it would be met and affirming my child as he is.

Sometimes Danny did things which exhibited his attempt to be the man of the house. He has frequently demonstrated to me various ways he would successfully fend off the "bad guys."

When I'm tired, sometimes Danny gently rubs my neck. It's tempting to really enjoy it and let him continue. But for me that is not a healthy choice. Instead, after about one minute, I hug him, thank him for his thoughtfulness and steer him in a different direction. It's crucial to affirm your children in their valiant efforts, yet to free them by your words and actions from their attempts to be a replacement spouse. I remind Danny how much I love him and appreciate him and also tell him that I don't expect him to be the daddy. I express my feelings of sadness and anger that Daddy is no longer here and tell him that it's OK for him to have these feelings too. Then I remind him that our heavenly Father watches over us and that I want him to enjoy being a little boy as long as he can.

At that point I suggest an activity we can do together. I read to him or we play a game, something where he reassumes his role as a child and where he sees that I'm the mom and we're going to be OK.

Looking back, I can see the development of a little tradition we call "Mommy/Danny time." Even now that he's growing up, he still asks for this time. I had to learn the importance of setting aside a little time each day (sometimes just ten to fifteen minutes) to give him my full attention. Whether we play or talk, it is precious time when we just enjoy each other. And when you're both seeking relief from pain, a moment of appreciation for your most special blessing can provide a ray of hope.

4. Can I allow myself to grieve for that "other child" I'll probably never have?

Perhaps you already had your desired number of children before your divorce. That was not the case for me.

For almost two years before Steve left, I was trying desperately to get pregnant again. My love for Danny was more than I had ever imagined, and I was so ready for another child.

Ever since I was little, I planned to have two children, a boy and a girl. Now that I had a boy, I would be happy with two boys, although I knew I would feel a loss if I never had a daughter.

Because of my age, combined with the likelihood that I'll not be remarrying anytime soon, it looks like Danny will be my only child. When this realization first hit me, I was gripped by three emotions:

- anger at Steve for obstructing the life of our future child by aborting our marriage;

- grief and sadness over the loss of the child that might have been;

- gratefulness for and passionate protectiveness toward the only child I'll ever have.

I had to remember that it's OK to cry. It's OK to grieve. Since I had already selected a boy's name and a girl's name, it was almost like the death of two real children. My children.

I wept before the Lord and tried to give back into His hands these children of my dreams.

All I could do was embrace the promises of His sovereignty and wisdom. I knew with my head long before I felt in my heart that He loves me more than I could ever imagine, and He does only what's best for His children. That includes me, Danny and my disappointed dreams. (See Daniel 4:35, Romans 8:28.)

God sees the whole picture, and He knows everything. He knew there was no way in the world I would have physically and emotionally been able to handle a baby or toddler during the divorce. He knew beforehand the tremendous strain I would be under in the next few years. He knew how much of my attention Danny would need.

After I grieve, I have to trust. And when the sadness wells up again I can grieve, and then I have to trust.

And I pray with all my heart that by God's grace I will be the very best parent in the whole world for the precious child He has given me.

5. How do I handle the mixture of feelings related to my children going over "there"?

Although the needs of our children will vary as they get older, our mothering instincts will always produce a desire to meet those needs. Whether it's being sure our toddler gets enough sleep or being concerned that our teen not succumb to peer pressure, we want to be there to provide, protect and guide.

Unfortunately, things come along which prevent us from doing this—such as divorce. Depending on the particulars of the settlement, many of us divorced women are only with our children a fraction of the time we used to be.

Just the fact that your child is away from you is difficult. Now divorce brings anger, pain, resentment and mistrust, making it very hard to let them go with their dad.

Every single time Danny drove off with Steve, I felt such a stinging emptiness, as if my child had been ripped right out of my womb. The ache was so overwhelming that it clouded my other feelings.

Now as I look back, I can identify each contributing component of this emotional mishmash: anger, jealousy, fear, grief and guilt.

The anger was the most apparent. It took me a long time to stop thinking, "It's not fair!" Steve was the one who left. Why should Danny and I suffer for his decision?

I was also jealous, mainly of Susan. This woman, who has only known my son for a few weeks, has now assumed a mother role toward him.

My feelings of fear were not totally unfounded and were closely tied in with loss of control. As far as I could tell, Steve did not care about Danny's sleep, nutrition, teeth and television input. Since Danny was only three-and-a-half-years old when Steve left, he was a long way from responsible decision making. I'm sure we could all share our horror stories of what goes on when the kids are with their dad. And there are usually consequences, unfortunately paid for by our children and by us.

Another feeling at seeing him go to his father's was grief. It was similar to leaving him on his first day of school, only deeper, because I knew it could have been prevented and it was not necessarily for his good. I am now missing out on part of his life. Although I encourage him to share with me when he gets back, Danny is not a talker. I felt sadness about the loss of this portion of Danny and his life that I will never know.

I've also struggled with guilt. With all of the other negative emotions flooding me at his weekly departure, there was this unfamiliar feeling of relief. Time alone, at last. Quietness. Freedom. And of course, instant guilt that I would dare enjoy the fact that Danny was away.

It was all so confusing, yet I was determined to sort through the feelings and grow, rather than just immediately numb the pain. I was often tempted to turn on the TV, but I realized that would only cause these feelings to fester, not make them go away. As with physical pain, emotional pain is there to tell us something is wrong and needs to be attended to before it worsens.

After working through the feelings (talking, writing, praying and listening to wise counsel), I have been able to let Danny go in peace. I remind myself of a few things when he goes:

- I do need time alone, and it is OK to enjoy the quiet and take time to play or rest.
- Steve is his father, whether I like it or not, and Danny needs his father.
- Although nobody on earth could ever be a better mother to Danny than I could, God loves him even more than I do.

6. How can I tell my non-Christian friends and family about the divorce without bringing dishonor to the Lord and shame on myself?

Because Steve had graduated from seminary and was involved in Christian ministry, it was no secret where he stood with his religious convictions. He had been a positive influence on many people over the years and was bold about sharing his beliefs with our non-Christian friends and relatives.

Exactly what happened over time to cause him to make the decisions he made, I may never fully understand. And that's OK because I realize now that I don't have to have all the answers.

But at the time, I wondered how to explain it to others.

My initial instinct was self-preservation. I wanted to be sure I emerged triumphant as the innocent victim. That mind-set paved the way for easy dumping. I figured he made the bad choices, why not just tell the truth. I could paint a pretty damaging portrait of Steve. But after a few times, I was not at all satisfied, and in fact, I felt even worse. Rather than elevating myself, I felt like part of me came down with him. I realized I needed to make a healthier choice in this area, one that contributed to rather than undermined my healing.

So as the pendulum swings, I switched my approach and gravitated toward Steve's defense. I didn't want the name of the Lord to be criticized and all the progress these people may have made in coming to Him to be wasted. It was difficult for me to isolate myself from Steve in this whole divorce situation, so making excuses for him seemed to help preserve my reputation at the same time.

But I couldn't honestly do this for long either. For me, it was unhealthy co-dependency to cover for Steve. I needed to separate myself, face the fact that he was gone and free myself from taking responsibility for his actions. As embarrassing as it felt at times, I was not responsible for what people thought and said about him.

As admirable as my concerns were for the Lord's reputation, He Himself was quite capable of handling that.

I realized I was responsible for *my* attitudes, actions and words. So as I focused on my conversations, there were three guidelines that were helpful:

- Keep talk about Steve to a minimum; acknowledge that God has given us all freedom of choice, and I don't have all the answers about Steve.

- As I talk about myself, stay transparent and try to be balanced. We're all capable of sin— it could just as easily have been me. Yes, there's pain and it's hard, but some days are better than others.

- Take advantage of each conversation as an opportunity to speak of the deep reality of God's promises. *He* is faithful, and we have much for which to be thankful and even more to look forward to.

7. What is the best way to adjust to the absence of a social life with other married couples?

Great! Yet another opportunity to demonstrate choice making! After realizing how much I missed this part of married life, I opted for the pity party. Woe is me—nobody wants a fifth wheel.

I'm learning that there's a fine line between feeling the feelings in a healthy way and feeling sorry for myself, which is actually feeding the feelings. It's a step toward healing to acknowledge the ache of loneliness and the pain of feeling left out. Then I must choose a good outlet to "work out" the garbage, such as talking with a caring listener, writing in my journal, going for a long walk, praying, crying. . . .

I may have to repeat the process again and again, but at least that prevents the toxic feelings from rotting and festering inside me.

Then I am free to make choices in moving on. I've been slow to jump into the singles scene, although there are some excellent Christian groups in our area. I've found joining a mixed group, with variety in age and marital status, to be the most helpful in meeting my social needs. Many churches have home Bible study groups which offer support, encouragement and fun times in a comfortable setting. In such groups people love and respect me for myself, not because of any particular role (wife, mother, etc.).

I also made a little extra effort to strengthen my friendship with other women—other mothers and some never-married women. I realized that although it's not the same as being a couple with other couples, we could have just as much fun.

Social life is not a luxury but a necessity. It's OK to play. It's OK to laugh.

And it sure feels good!

Reflection:

1. Evaluate your current relationship with your parents. What steps do you need to take to make that relationship healthier?

2. How do you feel toward your former in-laws, and how are you behaving toward them? What might you need to change?

3. How are you doing in the four areas of meeting your child's basic needs?

4. Have you allowed yourself to grieve for that child you may never have?

5. Describe your feelings as you watch your children drive off with him or as you drive away after dropping them off.

6. What is the healthiest way for you to tell others about the divorce? Write it out and practice saying it.

7. How are you responding to the changes in your social life? How can you initiate some social times with others this week?

Chapter 7

Memories: Dealing with Reminders

Sunday, the 12th

(Happy?) Mother's Day

Proverbs 3:5 "Trust in the Lord with all your heart and lean not on your own understanding."

I need to hold Your hand through this dark mess and follow You and trust You.

Saturday, the 8th

Went to the mall with Mom—I realized I'm not in pain constantly! Things remind me of Steve here and there, and that's hard.

But I'm so much freer than before, like a big heavy cloud is lifted!

Every year as Labor Day approaches, I am reminded that September 2 was our wedding day. January 23 is Steve's birthday. Every February 14 everyone else celebrates being in love, like we used to do. I hear songs on the radio or in stores that serenaded us as we fell in love. Yesterday a wedding invitation arrived in the mail.

Day after day, year after year, I'm stabbed with constant reminders of what once was and no longer is. Will each memory continue to stab me like a sharp knife blade, or will time bring healing and strength?

As I look to the Lord and continue to make healthy choices, I can anticipate with confidence that the wounds *will* heal, though they may always be tender.

1. As I force myself to sort through things loaded with memories, how do I release my feelings and how do I decide what to keep and what to burn?

It makes me sad to hear of ex-wives who, in a fit of anger, destroy all pictures and other memorable items of their marriage and former spouse. For one thing, they can never be duplicated. There's no going back if for some reason they ever regretted it.

But probably the most important reason to preserve photos and memorabilia is for the children. Regardless of the status of your relationship with their father, you and he will always be their parents. Pictures of the wedding and memories of happy days together will someday be invaluable and comforting to them. Should *they* choose to reject the memories, that will be their prerogative. *But they may never forgive you if you presume on their right to their heritage.*

I put away the pictures, framed certificates with our names, engraved items and other things that evoked strong memories. Emotionally, I knew I couldn't handle making any decisions at the time, and so I got the things out of sight to deal with later.

There have been times when I wanted to smash the fragile things to pieces, throw darts at his picture and much worse. One day shortly after he moved out, I threw a heart-shaped pin that said "I love Steve" at him and told him to give it to Susan.

Feelings of anger, pain and unfairness well up from my deepest parts as I see the sharp contrast of what was once my most beautiful dream come true, having now become my worst nightmare.

The pictures and mementos of trips and other special times we had together trigger a cognitive dissonance that screams, "What's wrong with this picture? How can this be? What happened?"

Unfortunately, it's another necessary step in the grieving process, a dark valley that has no healthy shortcuts.

I gave myself permission to deal with each memorable item when I felt ready. Some have been much more difficult than others: my wedding ring, wedding pictures, pictures of us together, memorable T-shirts, an engraved clock, an engraved stained-glass hanging, books stamped with our names, gifts he'd given me, things in the house or outside that we worked on together, wedding gifts, my wedding dress, honeymoon and vacation souvenirs, and of course, the ultimate reminder—our son.

Some things caused me to weep as I simultaneously faced the memory and the decision of what to do with it. A few items I've been able to give away.

To be honest with you, there are also several things I still haven't faced. The wedding dress is still hanging in my mother's closet. The pictures I'll always keep because I know Danny will want them someday. I'm OK with those now, because I've gone back through them and grieved. I can move ahead.

And there's the stained-glass hanging with our names and wedding date. Several times I've almost smashed it on the ground, but couldn't. I don't know what I'll do with it or when. But when the time is right, I'll know. For now, it's put away in a closet.

Each person will have her own memorable items and her own best timeline for sorting through them. My words of encouragement are twofold:

- It's OK to cry or yell or feel whatever you are feeling. Remember to process the emotions in a constructive way.

- Take your time. Don't act out of spite. You can always give or throw things away at a later date, but you can never bring them back once they've been destroyed.

These memories represent a significant part of your life. Just because your ex-husband is no longer part of your life does not nullify what you had. We don't need to throw away the past just because it holds no future.

You are on your way to healing when you can embrace those memories as once very real, a part of who you are. At the same time you must release your expectation that to be valid they should have continued unbroken. The balance is tricky: You don't have to reject the memories because he is gone, but you must come to the point where you aren't dependent on the past. Pack them up as an extension of you, and begin to take your next step toward becoming the beautiful person God is forming.

2. Will the pain of each holiday gradually go away, or can I do something to help?

Yes and yes. Although each person and her circumstances will vary, as long as you apply the steps for survival listed in Chapter 1, time will bring healing. It will take more time for some than others. But there *is* hope. It *will* get better.

In the meantime, in addition to processing your feelings in a healthy way, there are a few things you might consider as these inevitable holidays roll around.

First, be careful not to dwell on the past. As memories and their accompanying feelings crop up, let them come. Feel the ache and the sting and all that comes with them. When you feel a lull, take advantage of that crucial point to choose between staying there and soaking in the muck or taking a step ahead toward cleansing. As you give yourself a healthy outlet for those feelings, the pain won't totally disappear, but you will be moving in the right direction.

Another thought has been helpful to me, but because I'm not as creative as others, the progress has been slow. On the holidays that I must continue to observe (now without a husband), I try to establish new traditions. It has been helpful to talk with other wives and mothers to get ideas and also to brainstorm a little with Danny. The purpose here is to get the focus off of what no longer is and pave the way to building *new* memories.

For instance, instead of counting my Valentines (wow, one from my mother), Danny and I could make a card and some cookies to take to a lonely person at the nearby nursing home. With joint custody, Danny splits the celebration of certain holidays between me and Steve. So we have had to come up with special ways to have Christmas and birthdays, even when they are not on the actual day. I've learned that's OK too.

Whatever I can do to refocus and begin to build new memories will, in time, help transform a day of painful reminders into a day of pleasant memories.

3. Can I prepare myself in advance for the things that will catch me off guard and trigger negative emotions?

One week after Steve moved out, he bought a new Jeep Cherokee. From then on, every time I saw a gray Jeep Cherokee I felt like puking. Sometimes I also felt like jamming my foot on the accelerator and smashing into it. Or speeding past and giving them a dirty look or choice words. All this from sweet little me.

Steve used to drive the city transit buses. It took me a couple of years to not react every time I saw one. In that case, it was probably the frequency that helped desensitize me eventually.

On several occasions I've been thrown off guard by music in the grocery store. I know the music is intended to put you in a good mood so you'll buy more. Well, they didn't count on emotionally exposed women recovering from divorce. The Christmas right after he left was the worst. I was at the supermarket in the detergent aisle. "I'll Be Home for Christmas" began playing. I was paralyzed as I leaned over my grocery cart, sobbing. He would not be home for Christmas. He would never again be home for Christmas.

I don't know if I can honestly say there's a sure-fire way to be prepared for these surprises. But I have learned a few things that have helped.

When possible, avoid places and things that trigger the pain. It would be masochistic for me to deliberately go where I knew I'd have to see his car or to a memorable location. I'm also taking a foolish risk by tuning in to the local mellow-music oldies radio station.

After doing what I can to avoid the memory triggers, it has also been helpful to maintain my survival checklist explained in Chapter 1. Keeping those "tools" current allows me to draw on them at any time, especially when I'm caught off guard by circumstances.

The most crucial thing I can do as I progress from surviving to growing is to walk with the Lord. That involves a conscious awareness of who He is and the importance of a daily relationship with Him. Reading the Bible and praying are vital components of this walk. One of my barometers that indicates how well I'm doing is how long it takes me to turn to the Lord in a time of need. Just last night after receiving a very painful phone call, I stood dazed in the hallway. I battled the urge to turn on the TV and start munching. I remembered to feel the feelings. And then I prayed.

Ideally, I would like to instinctively turn to the Lord for help first whether I need to cry before Him, knowing He cares, or whether I need wisdom for a situation. I know He is always there, waiting for me, and I am learning to go to Him more quickly.

When my walk with the Lord is honest and growing, I can reach out to Him any time. He is not caught off guard by anything. And He will help me through.

A sign on my refrigerator says, "Fear not tomorrow; God is already there."

4. When will I be able to tolerate sentimental music?

It took me a long time to be able to listen to romantic music and actually enjoy it. There were many times when I'd turn on the radio only to have my heart wrenched by some memorable love song. Sometimes I knew I needed to cry and this was the ideal catalyst. Other times I took control and quickly switched stations or turned it off.

As a music lover, this has been a difficult area for me. During the time when I wasn't yet ready to listen to my old favorites, there were a few things I was able to do which helped. My first remedy was to fill the void with good Christian music. I had not kept up with what was out there and was pleasantly surprised. Not only is the music pleasurable as I listen, but it's uplifting. I come away a little stronger and with a renewed perspective. When I get my mind focused on Jesus, there is hope.

Another helpful strategy has been to expose myself to new music, whether Christian or secular. New songs and new styles of music can be enjoyable and culturally expanding.

Finally, a strategy which requires time: Create new associations with the old favorites to replace the past memories. This may only work for some people, and it will take time, new experiences and maybe new people in order to establish the associations. For example, when I used to hear Barry Manilow sing "Looks Like We Made It," I'd remember the summer before Steve and I were married when we were apart for eight weeks and thought we'd never survive. Now, I use this song at the end of my exercise tape to congratulate myself for making it through the workout.

5. What's the best way to survive going to a wedding?

The first wedding I had to attend after the divorce was a killer. At one point I was crying my heart out. At another point it was all I could do to keep from standing up and shouting, "Don't believe him! Run now while you still have a chance!"

As much as I tried to ignore my own past and celebrate with these newlyweds, I couldn't. I felt like a sitting target with memory missiles aimed directly at me. As each one struck me, I felt bursts of pain. Anger. Loneliness. Cynicism. Hatred. Loss. Grief. It was almost like attending a baby dedication after losing your own child.

I felt like the biggest hypocrite. What in the world was *I* doing here? Marriage was the last thing I had faith in. I had been where they were once, and look where it got me. Yet here I was all dressed up with an approving veneer smile, masking the remains of my half of a dead marriage.

In order to survive, I had to adhere to two key guidelines: Feel the feelings and make healthy choices.

About two years after the divorce, I attended another wedding. I looked great and felt great. Until the music started. My left brain dominated as I told myself, "I'm fine, I'm healed, and I'm excited for my friends." That worked for about ten minutes, and then the right brain levy broke and the floods came. I realized I needed to let the feelings rise to the surface. I am not super-single-woman, and I may never be 100 percent over Steve. It's OK to hurt, and it's necessary to cry.

I received a wedding invitation last week. As a choice maker, I've learned that I can say no. If I feel it will stir up more pain and it is best not to go, then I decline.

Yet I am also free to choose to go, to choose to support and celebrate with my friends. It would not be healthy for me to nurse my bitterness by whining, "It's not fair. If I can't be happily married, nobody else can either." In essence, that's what my skepticism says.

There is a good chance that the other couple *will* be happy, and I choose to cheer them on. I also choose not to allow my disappointments and my marital corpse to spoil their hopes and dreams.

And just between us, deep down inside I have that same hope and dream, to live happily ever after once again.

Reflection:

1. What memorable items do you still need to face? When you are ready, how will you process your feelings?

2. Which holidays are most difficult for you? What can you do in advance to survive and to make new memories?

3. What do you tend to do to cover up painful feelings? Name one healthy thing you can do immediately the next time you get caught off guard emotionally.

4. How do you respond when you hear love songs?

5. If you've been to a wedding recently, describe your feelings. If not, how will you know when you are ready to attend a wedding?

Chapter 8

Work: On the Job and at Home

Tuesday, the 14th

Nervous about finances—I'm getting hit hard this month, to say nothing of the $10,000 attorney fees!

Oh Lord. Here we go again. "I don't know about tomorrow . . ." but I know You.

Although each person arrives at the toll bridge of divorce in a different car, everybody pays. Divorce sucks most people dry and usually results in a major upheaval of one's previous financial situation. Depending on the specific terms of the settlement, in addition to the usual bills, you will likely be dealing with spousal support and/or child support, legal fees, the entire rent or house payment, debts, child care and a need for more income fast.

With one less husband around, we as ex-wives are left with the burden of having to work more, both outside the home and around the house.

1. How can I best deal with my new financial circumstances?

Because I am not a financial counselor, I can't give you any easy answers. But because I've been where you are, I can share things which have been helpful to me.

The first step I recommend is to find a wise and trustworthy financial advisor. This could be a friend or family member, or it could be a reputable professional. He or she can objectively assess your situation and offer some helpful suggestions.

Consider talking with your pastor or an elder at your church. Not only is it important that they be aware of your situation, but also they may have some practical ideas and words of wisdom. It was always an encouragement to me when one of the leaders of my church would ask me how I was do-

ing financially. Not only was there genuine concern, but they were prepared with some resources
if necessary.

There are additional resources for people with
economic hardships. Books and tapes are plenti-
ful. Check your local Christian bookstore, li-
brary and general bookstore. Depending on your
situation, there is a variety of government programs for which you may qualify. Also, some
communities sponsor "gleaning" programs
where surplus food and supplies are distributed
to struggling families.

Another necessary but usually dreaded step is
to make a budget. Yuk. I just hate that word. It's
so confining. When I forced myself to go
through my checkbook and write down everything I spend each month, it was eye-opening.
Also depressing. But at least I knew the reality
of what I was dealing with and had a point from
which to start.

Part of the budgeting process has been to force
myself to discern between needs and wants. I've
had to tighten up since the divorce, and it hasn't
been fun. It has taken sheer discipline and a conscious retraining when I'm in the store. Sometimes I know it is not even wise for me to go
inside certain stores—particularly shoes and clothing—unless I've determined previously what I
specifically need and am disciplined enough to
stick to my list.

Where children are involved, it may also be
appropriate to discuss the budget in general

terms, emphasizing the importance of financial responsibility. As situations arise, you can learn together to discern between needs and wants and to help each other be accountable for wise spending.

Finally, pray for wisdom. James 1:5 promises that when we ask God for wisdom, He will give it. I'm learning to seek His wisdom in every area of my life, and the area of money gives me a daily opportunity to do so.

2. Can I balance the practical and emotional issues related to my now having to work?

There's something inside me that cries out in rebellion when anybody tells me I *have* to do something. It could be a diet with strict guidelines about what and how much to eat; it could be a bell signaling the beginning of a class; it could be Danny's school telling us we have to sell candy for a fund-raiser. Or it could be, and now actually is, the world telling me I have to go back to work.

I began working full time right out of college the week after we were married. Teaching school for seven years was stressful for me, and I dreamed of the day when I could stay home and be a mommy. For another two years, I enjoyed playing around with some other careers, including receptionist, college instructor and activity director for seniors. Although it was a nice break from teaching grade school, the cloud of "having to work" still lingered.

Finally Steve finished school, and my dream began to come true. I got pregnant with Danny and stopped working. We bought our first house. Danny was born, and I was able to stay home with him.

I taught piano lessons from home, which provided extra spending money. But work was fun because I could stay home.

I loved being home. I loved having time to be with my son, to watch him, to nurture him and to enjoy him. I loved being my own boss. I loved cooking, cleaning and even laundry. And I loved the freedom to come and go as I pleased.

All this came to a screeching halt with the divorce. Finances dictated that I get a job. And that required a whole new wardrobe. (Tennis shoes and sweats weren't quite corporate enough.)

I hated Steve for this annihilation of my dream-come-true life. I hated the alarm clock for its daily rude awakening. I hated blow dryers, makeup, nylons and uncomfortable shoes. I hated commuter traffic. I hated fluorescent lights and stale office air. I hated the miniscule paycheck that was left after taxes and expenses.

But more than anything, it tore my heart apart to leave Danny at day-care. He was my son, and I should be able to be with him. And when I picked him up, I was tired and he was angry. This was so wrong. This was not the way things were supposed to turn out.

Now that he's in school, that part is easier. But I still struggle with anger and resentment that I can't do what I want to do with my time. Had we

WORK: ON THE JOB AND AT HOME   127

still been married, I might have worked part time to earn extra income for home improvements or Danny's college. Or I would have been able to be more involved at church or as a volunteer.

But I'm not, and I've had to accept that this is the way it is. Maybe not forever, but for now.

I need to keep current with my negative feelings so that resentment doesn't build. Each day as I back the car out of the garage, I commit my work to the Lord. I pray for wisdom and direction.

As I go up three flights of stairs to the office, I pray for strength and a good attitude. Every day I need to do this.

I thank God for my job and for my health. And I trust Him that even though this is not my choice, this is where He has put me for now.

He will bless me as I walk with Him through the valleys of disappointment. He will bring beautiful things out of all of this as I keep my eyes on Him.

3. What is the least awkward and most socially acceptable way to tell my co-workers and supervisor about my situation?

In arriving at the best answer to this, you'll want to ask yourself what you want them to know and why. Carefully select a mature person and only disclose the main facts, basically that you are now divorced.

What you say will all depend on your relationship with your boss and co-workers and also whether or not this is a new job. In some cases, it would not be necessary or appropriate to bring it up. Other situations will warrant a personal disclosure. If you choose to tell someone, be sure it is to the person(s) who need to know this turn of events in your life. It will probably be just a matter of time before it becomes common knowledge, so let it run its course.

Not only is it wise to be discreet about *who* you tell, choose carefully *what* you tell. Your workplace is not a counseling center, and you're not after pity or sympathy. You'll avert some of the criticism and gossip by keeping your story brief. Remember why you want them to know. It's safest to stay in the left brain with a simple update of "just the facts, ma'am."

I would also encourage you to include some type of reassurance, to the effect that this change in your personal life will not interfere with your job. This could include letting the boss know you have found dependable child care, will not be receiving numerous calls from your children, ex-husband or lawyers and that you have found someone other than co-workers to talk to who will guide you through this transition in your life.

4. Is it possible to continue doing a good job without allowing my emotional ups and downs to affect me at work?

Depending on your work setting and job description, some days will be tougher than others.

There have been times when it's all I could do to choke back the tears, and other times when I was so angry I wanted to scream,

The good news is that I've found a few things that have helped. First, although it's not always possible to anticipate the people or things that will pierce my composure, I can be on the alert for certain predictable "enemies" that can wear down my defenses. For instance, at PMS time, my nerves are raw, yet I have the advantage of knowing those days ahead of time. Perhaps rainy days, an upcoming anniversary for a co-worker, an office party with spouses or a certain customer can rub you the wrong way. Like taking extra vitamins when I feel a cold coming on, it's been helpful to me to put a little extra effort into my survival checklist during these times.

Another strategy for maintaining my composure as I try to focus on my work has been to modify the "feel the feelings" guideline. As painful, negative, anti-productive feelings emerge at inconvenient times, I've learned to push the "pause" button. This can be tricky, because we may flirt with the temptation to repress the feelings. It's unhealthy to say, "I can't handle this feeling now, and if I stifle it, it will go away." But since we know feelings never go away until they are processed, the goal here is to consciously acknowledge the pain and put it on hold until later in the day when you can release it freely. Then you must be sure to deal with it as soon as possible, which for me is usually through crying and writing.

Most of us have times when we just need to be alone. This is especially important during emotionally taxing times. Find your own private getaway where you can retreat from work when you need to have some space. For some it means going to the car for lunch or other breaks. For others, it may mean finding a vacant room or closing the office door. A bathroom stall might work or a bathroom on another floor where you are less likely to see someone you know. Find what works for you, and take advantage of it when necessary.

Although I have not personally encountered co-workers who are bitter toward men, they are not uncommon in some work settings. Visualize a group of women getting together for a coffee break in the lunch room. Invariably there will be a few "man haters" in the crowd who love to talk about how badly they were treated during their divorce, what a rat their ex-husband is, how all men are creeps and can't be trusted, ad nauseam. They will tell you that you are in good company and did the right thing by ditching the bum. This will add fuel to the fire already burning within you, and for a while, it may satisfy you to exchange stories of how bad men and marriage can be. While it may be tempting to swap stories of "How I Have Been Wronged," in the end it will make you feel worse. I'm sure these women all mean well, but they are not processing their pain and disappointment in a way God honors. I make it a point to steer clear of these women as much as possible, because they can be poison to the woman who is seeking to rebuild her life using godly principles.

Treat yourself with something you can look at on your desk or wall that will make you feel good. How about a tiny stuffed animal or fresh flowers in a pretty vase? I love plants, and I find myself refreshed when I consciously stop and appreciate them. Even subconsciously, a cheery reminder that you are special can do wonders. A beautiful scenic picture on my office wall helps me relax and readjust my perspective by carrying me away to the peaceful solitude of a mountain lake.

Please give yourself the freedom to do the best you can do. None of us is super-employee. One day at a time and as unto the Lord. He knows. And He cares.

5. How do I deal with the extra work load around the house?

I was fortunate to have a husband who was capable of fixing anything around the house and handling what I categorized the "man-type" duties. As I'm faced with things that need repair or routine maintenance, I'm usually plagued with one of two emotions: anger and resentment at the extra work which Steve dumped on me or a fearful feeling of helplessness, not even having a clue where to begin.

Taking care of the car wasn't such a burden, because I knew there were places to take it. Some of the things that have thrown me for a loop were the stupid lawn mower that wouldn't start, assembling a new vacuum cleaner, putting up a new pull-down shade, trying to nab the mole that was constructing subways below our lawn and attempting to fix every broken toy and bike Danny has brought to me. The list will continue until I retire to a nursing home.

After the usual recommended therapy of screaming, yelling, saying a few naughty words and crying, I decided perhaps this was an area about which I could actually do something. My first step was to acquire my own set of tools, which (bless her heart) my mom sent me at Christmas. Not very exciting, I'll admit, but a lifesaver. (They were in a cute red box, which helped.)

Now that I was equipped to handle anything, my next step was to be willing to try. Just try. What do we have to lose? But be forewarned, we have to be prepared to laugh at ourselves. And for our kids to laugh too.

Here's what I mean. Shortly after I received my new cool tool kit, I had an opportunity to try it out. Danny's remote control for his race car had stopped working, and he asked me to fix it. Intelligent sleuth that I am, I deduced that the battery must be dead and proudly announced that I would change it. Simple. Just unscrew the screw that held the battery case, replace the battery and screw it shut.

It didn't take long for me to get frustrated, wondering why none of my screwdrivers worked. I tried every one, from every imaginable angle, every direction. Wouldn't budge. Disappointed, I surrendered, telling Danny I was sorry and that we'd let Daddy fix it.

When Steve came over the next day, I tried to impress him by showing him my tool kit and all the effort we'd made to loosen the screw. He just stood there and laughed, which didn't help. It was at that moment I realized I had to make a choice: Be defensive and resentful and feel like a failure, or be willing to learn and laugh at my mistakes because I am OK, with or without tools.

I could actually laugh when Steve pointed out that the "screw" was just a superficial design on the plastic, and all I had to do was slide the cover off.

Because I've been willing to attempt some of these unfamiliar tasks, I have come away rewarded. I usually learn something new (never too old), and when the job is successful, I feel I've really accomplished something. In more cases than not, the experience is a boost to my self-esteem, and I feel more confident in my ability to handle the next challenge.

There have been other times when I have done my best, unfortunately to no avail. At that point I've given myself permission to ask someone to show me how to do it. That way I learn and am able to do it next time.

Another part of surviving the extra work load around the house is knowing when to ask someone else to do a job. I know there are some tasks that, whether or not I *could* do them, it would not be wise for me to try. These are things that could be dangerous or cause injury (lifting heavy objects, electrical work, roof work) or tasks that I could not afford to mess up (such as plumbing).

Take up any freebie offers that have been extended to you. There may be someone in the neighborhood or at church who would love to help out. I had a neighbor family offer their help if I "ever needed anything."

At first I felt guilty and uncomfortable about calling them. But I reminded myself that people usually do want to help, and they wouldn't have offered if they didn't mean it. So Dave, formerly just a neighbor, has now been promoted to be my official lawn mower troubleshooter. And I really appreciate him.

Finally, there will be tasks for which you'll have to hire someone. Ideally, it would be great to have a capable, versatile handyman on whom to call for a variety of odd jobs. A word to the wise here: You may have to go through a few before you find a good one. Look for someone who has been referred to you and someone who isn't trying to put the moves on you. (I had to go through four before I found one with both a good head and a good heart.)

Do what you can, delegate what you can't, and as you pound in that nail, you can sing out: "I am woman, hear me roar!"

Reflection:

1. Pray for an objective financial advisor if you don't have one. Make a budget if you have not already done so.

2. If your work situation has changed, how have you processed your feelings about it?

3. If you haven't already done so, decide who at work you need to tell about the divorce and write out what you will say.

4. What is the best way for you to handle your emotional ups and downs at work?

5. How do you feel when you attempt to do something you've never done before and you succeed? Begin a list of resources for each area you may need help with (car, yard work, appliance repair, etc.).

Chapter 9

Church: Who Am I and Why Am I Here?

Friday, the 5th

I can't do it, Lord. I'm sick. I'm tired. I'm ready to beat Danny and scream. I just want to get away and be alone. I'm ready to snap.

Lord, show me that either You will help me continue this ministry, or else help me break it off.

I don't have to be invincible. Everyone is admiring my faith and faithfulness, but I can't live up to the expectations of others.

It hurts. But I have the rest of my life for that. Now I must survive, for me and for Danny.

With all the changes in my life and being single again, church feels like a different place. It's much more awkward than being a newcomer, because at least guests are usually warmly welcomed and directed to the group of people where they'd feel most comfortable.

As I progress through this period of readjustment, many issues have arisen: my identity and sense of belonging, how to relate to people now that I'm divorced, how they relate to me, my role in ministry and the wide range of feelings I experience every Sunday.

1. Who do I tell about my situation, and how much should I share?

Since every church is different, the answer depends on the size of the congregation, who you know and how well you know them. Another factor to consider is why you want to tell them. Is it a need on your part to open up and share your pain? Do you just want people to be informed of the basics of the situation? Do you want them to hear your side to minimize gossip? Or do you want them to pray for you?

After you discern why you want to share, then it will be easier to decide to whom you should talk and with how much detail.

By the time my divorce was final, almost everybody already knew my situation. I had chosen to go to my pastor and his wife first. They were very

supportive and also respected my confidentiality
until I requested that others be informed.

From the very beginning, I also shared with my
ensemble and choir. These were my friends, and I
desperately needed their support and prayers.
Some very special people were with me the whole
way through and are still there when I need them.
There were a few people with whom I shared
everything, because I needed to unload and I
knew they cared.

With others, I came prepared weekly with a
brief update in answer to their frequent, "How are
you?" I appreciated their asking but chose to keep
it simple.

*2. How can I learn to reach out and receive support
from the right people when I need it, yet protect myself
from the "energy-drainers" who mean well but aren't
helpful?*

I felt so good when I saw certain people approach me at church, but there were also a few
who made me wish I had gone out the other door.

I remember one woman who asked me how I
was doing. Not having the energy that day to talk
to her, I answered, "Pretty good, thanks." Appar-
ently she wasn't satisfied. She took my arm, got in
my face and asked, "How are you *really*?"

I put her in the category of energy-drainers.
These are the people who leave you worse off after their interaction than you were before. They
selfishly suck out what little strength you may

have left. With the exception of a few who are just nosey, most are probably well-meaning. Unfortunately, they usually approach you with no clue as to where you are emotionally. It is up to you to identify them and then make a choice as to the healthiest way to respond.

I go out of my way to avoid offending others. Some of you may be like me. We give of ourselves to keep people happy. To a certain extent, that is admirable; but if taken to an extreme, it is unhealthy.

Remember the boundaries. You are in one of the most painful, heart-wrenching, stressful times of your life right now. Survival is your goal. Please allow yourself to take the necessary steps to survive. It's OK to take care of yourself.

Most Sundays I arrive at church tired, both physically and emotionally depleted. I desperately need a refill in the form of comfort, hope and encouragement. Sometimes I just need a safe place for a cleansing cry as I pour out my grief before the Lord. Since I come with nothing to give, I need supporters, not energy-drainers.

I have learned to be brief, but gracious, with those who are not helpful. At times it was difficult, but I learned not to stop—to keep walking as I spoke.

It was also important for me to identify my needs each week and to seek out the best person to help. Sometimes this required a direct request, and sometimes all I needed was to come in contact with the person. In time, I knew who would be

there for me and in what capacity. My list of
needs led me to select my favorite supporters:

- Someone to pray with me
- Someone to regularly pray for me
- Someone to care
- Someone to listen
- Someone to hug me
- Someone to fix something around the house
- Someone to send me a card of encourage-
    ment
- Someone I can call any time
- Someone to have me over
- Someone to laugh and play with
- Someone to ask for advice
- Someone to help with Danny

As for the woman who got in my face, she may
still be wondering how I'm *really* doing. And
that's OK with me.

3. To which class or social group do I now belong?

My identity at this church had always been as
Steve's wife and Danny's mom. For years we par-
ticipated in activities for families and married couples.

Now I was suddenly single again, but won-
dered if I'd ever really *feel* single. I didn't feel comfortable switching over to the singles' group.

Ironically, I felt I had nothing in common with them. I also wondered if it might be too soon, as if I were "entering the market" before the dust even settled on Steve's favorite chair.

I desperately needed to belong somewhere, but because I was confused about my own identity and needs, I didn't know where to go.

Hindsight always offers such seemingly simple solutions. As I look back now, the best thing for me to do would have been to identify my needs and then find the best group to meet them. (As you read on, I encourage you to make your own list of what you need right now from a church group or class.) Finally it occurred to me to ask myself what I was seeking. I came up with the following needs:

- To be accepted and affirmed for who I am as a person
- To be wanted and included
- To belong; to identify with a group
- To receive spiritual support
- To laugh and play and participate in social events

Once I had consciously thought these through, I was able to seek the best group for me.

Since everybody's needs are different and the chemistry of each group is unique, it may take some looking to find the group where you feel most comfortable.

For me, it was a weekly fellowship group of mixed ages and marital status. I was able to re-establish my identity and receive affirmation for just being me. We've had some great Bible studies and some enjoyable social times. It has felt good to belong, to be wanted and to be encouraged not as a single or as a divorcee, but as *me*.

Overtime, I have gradually become more comfortable participating in Christian singles' functions in our city.

4. How do I respond when there's a sermon on marriage, and how do I process my cynical feelings as I observe all the happily married couples?

Hearing a sermon on marriage, I feel awkward and embarrassed. I might as well be a blind person attending a photography class. Certainly everyone can see the fluorescent sign over my head that says, "Not Married." Then it flashes, "She had her chance." The real blow comes when the subject is divorce. Was I aware that God hates divorce and it is not an option for the Christian? Ouch.

Over time, it has gotten easier. I am learning to bravely look back and identify the areas where I was weak and to begin to forgive Steve for his shortcomings. I am learning to accept that God loves me and I am precious to Him regardless of my marital status. And I am learning to optimistically peek ahead to those things I'll need should I remarry someday.

In spite of these growth steps, as I see married couples coming and going to church or sitting close together during a service, unpleasant feelings well up inside of me. I usually have three complaints:

- "It's not fair." (envy)
- "It's just an act." (mistrust)
- "It won't last." (pessimism)

These ugly feelings can spoil a good church service. When I am walking closely with the Lord, He quickly causes me to be aware of my bitterness. Once I'm conscious of these thoughts, I can deal with them.

There are four things I am learning to do when I catch myself in this frame of mind. (And I have to repeat these steps the next week or the next day or five minutes later.)

First, I have to pray, asking the Lord to show me which thoughts are wrong. My feelings are not necessarily sin. It's what I *do* with them that determines right or wrong. When I begin with a feeling of envy and then continue to dwell on it and cultivate it, that is sin. There was a point at which *feeling* the feeling crossed over the line to *feeding* the feeling. I have to acknowledge my bad choice and ask the Lord to take it away, to forgive and cleanse me.

Then I have to accept the facts and let go. I remind myself to be compassionate toward those who may be stuck in a bad marriage. I give thanks that I'm not. I can pray for them. As my own healing progresses, I am able to do that more.

Finally, I try to be happy for those who do have good marriages. "Rejoicing with those who rejoice" demonstrates selflessness to the extent that I don't allow my problems to poison someone else's joy. I can forget myself long enough to vicariously feel their happiness. And in the long run it all comes back for my own encouragement. There is hope. Good marriages do exist.

5. What is the healthiest way to handle all of the guilt-inflicting, painful comments from well-meaning Christians?

Whether they were intending to make me feel better or to give me hope or to steer me on the "right" track, too many thoughtless people gave me their "two cents" worth. Although I would have felt better had they kept silent, I might have missed the opportunity to face their challenges.

You may have received some of the following comments that to me seemed self-righteous, unfounded and irritating.

- "It's God's will for you to be together; divorce is not an option for Christians."
- "If you just pray and believe, Steve will come back."
- "Just be faithful and he'll come back."
- "I know God will bring him back."
- "Steve and Susan's relationship won't last."

- "Has he come back yet?"
- "Would you take him back?"
- "Are you willing to wait?"

The healthiest way for me to respond in each situation was to attempt to discern the wisdom from the humanistic input. From there I gracefully discarded the worthless comments and pursued the valuable comments.

It was important for me to remember to be aware of my feelings (resentment, anger, guilt, sadness or a literal chill up my spine) and to process them appropriately. I wanted to be willing to listen and learn, yet to reserve the right to sort it through later as I prayed for God's wisdom.

At the time of the question or comment, my immediate objective was to provide a polite, neutral response designed to bring a close to the conversation: "Thank you. I appreciate your prayers."

Yet if my interpretation of Scripture differed significantly and I had the energy, sometimes I challenged what they said: "I realize one marriage was God's ideal design, but unfortunately we are sinners and don't always make the best choices." And again, "We always appreciate your prayers."

Later I was able to reflect on the comments. Some prompted deep reflection on the issues brought up. But I had to come to the point where I realized again that I am a choice maker. After listening openly to what was shared, I am free to decide what to claim as truth and what to discard.

This attitude helps me to be willing to hear what people want to say without allowing them to dictate my response. When my defensive feelings are out of the way, I am no longer plagued by false guilt, and I am more receptive to what is true.

6. How can I take advantage of church as a time and place to process my feelings, to heal and to refocus?

During and after the divorce, church became a different place for me. Now, more than just a weekly spiritual shot in the arm and social hour, it was my eagerly anticipated haven. In addition to the encouraging words and hugs, it offered an hour to think, to feel deeply and to get a fresh glimpse of the Lord.

Not that I couldn't get all this at other times during the week, but when one is starving, a hearty meal served on a silver platter is not to be taken for granted. All I had to do was take my hungry, hurting heart and go.

On the way, I tried to remember to pray for a receptive spirit so I would hear what the Lord wanted me to. I prayed that my eyes would be on Him and that I would regain true perspective.

There were some days when I just needed to be alone, to think, to pray and to cry. It took me awhile to realize that was OK. The first thing I had to do was invest in some waterproof mascara for Sundays. I also knew on certain days that it was important for me not to have Danny with me. There will be times when you need to put the children in their classes, whether or not they want to go. That break for you is absolutely essential.

On these days, which were quite frequent, I made it a point to sit alone or near someone I did not know. I didn't want to have to talk to anyone or explain anything. I also found it helpful to leave before the last song ended so I could get out without talking to anyone.

It goes back again to being a choice maker. What do I have to do to survive? What do I need right now? Some of you may have just the opposite need. You may need people most when you're hurting. You'll find you need to sit with someone you know and may even want to arrange it the night before so you know someone will be looking out for you. You may find it's easier to feel and heal and hear what the Lord has for you when you're not alone.

Often what I needed to hear came in the form of music. Sometimes it was through the testimony of someone else who was struggling. Other times it was through the sermon or Scripture. But without fail, my pain, as real as it was, became bearable in light of God's promises and other peoples' struggles.

The feelings I experienced at church always seemed so much more intense. The deep grief, loneliness and hurt were surrounded by even bigger comfort and love. Glimpses of hope occasionally penetrated to a depth I could feel but not verbalize. The moments of praise and worship I experienced also were much deeper. My reasons for joy and rejoicing are no longer based on temporary, superficial circumstances. I can praise because of who the Lord is and all He's been to me in my pain.

And I come away feeling cleansed, peaceful and with a healthier perspective. God's Word is true, and He is faithful. All I need to do is walk one step at a time with my hand in His.

7. Am I less spiritual because I feel the need to take a leave of absence from my current ministry? How will I know when I'm ready again to give to others?

For the first year after Steve's departure, I stuck with my singing group ministry. Although it required time and commitment, I came out way ahead. I desperately needed these people for support, and the music was always uplifting.

But finally it got to the point where I was making sacrifices I couldn't afford. The accumulation of stress and the developments of the divorce left me physically and emotionally depleted. I had to ask myself if this ministry was building me up or wearing me down. And I dreaded the answer.

I needed to begin with priorities. With so many increasing demands now as a single parent, I've found it easy to let the list of things to do dictate my activities. I still need to pause periodically to evaluate the importance of these activities. My top priority will always be the Lord and my relationship with Him. Next is myself and my family. My job, church and other things come after that.

Once I realized that my relationship with the Lord did not depend on how much I was doing for Him, I was able to focus on the foremost task He's given me: caring for my family (Danny).

I was spending time and energy on this singing ministry, time which I desperately needed to spend at home. My health was not good. Danny's emotions were unstable. It was clear that I had to make this decision, but it was very, very difficult.

As I now examine the reasons that beckoned me to continue, I can see that my motives and priorities were mixed up. I now recognize five fears that almost prevented me from taking a much-needed leave of absence:

- Fear of being a failure; not being able to keep a commitment because of weakness
- Fear that the need I was meeting in that ministry now won't get met
- Fear of what others would think
- Fear of missing out
- Fear of losing my friends and support group

I had to work through each one of these, mostly over the phone with my mom. Once I had reassurance that these fears were far outweighed by my need to survive this crisis, then I was able to grant myself permission to take a break. This decision would not make me a failure, but rather a wise choice maker during this stressful time. Because I chose to limit my activities, I was able to survive. I also humbly realized that God can continue to work without me. Maybe this would even allow someone else an opportunity to receive the blessing of being used. And although I might miss out, I could still stay in regular contact with my special friends.

I reminded myself that my leave of absence was temporary. I would be back. Moses, Paul and even Jesus needed time out in the wilderness. God knows our needs and has never asked us to be superhuman. I couldn't do it, and that was OK.

When I began considering coming back into ministry again, there were a few things that helped me through the transition. First, I took as much time off as I needed and then started in slowly. One small commitment first. See how it goes. Give it plenty of time. Then be available for more, as the *Lord* leads.

Second, I continually checked my motives. Why am I doing this? Am I just afraid to say no? Or am I ready to minister to others again?

God can use people in pain. In fact, with the exception of Jesus, He only uses imperfect people. If I wait until I'm totally healed and never make any more mistakes, it (ministry) won't ever happen. But as I make myself available, God will lead me and use me just as I am.

Reflection:

1. What are your greatest needs right now as you go to church each week?

2. Name your favorite supporters. How do you communicate to them when you have a need?

3. How do you feel about your identity at church? If you are not satisfied, what steps can you take toward a healthier identity?

4. How can you prepare yourself to benefit from the next sermon on marriage?

5. Recall a hurtful comment that someone made to you recently. What did you feel? How could you best respond in a healthy way if you hear it again?

6. What is the best preparation for you to allow yourself the maximum benefit from church this Sunday?

7. Take a moment to evaluate your involvement at church or other "giving" ministries: Is this activity building you up or draining you? Would it be wise to consider some time off temporarily? How will you know when you're ready to resume it again?

Chapter 10

His Remarriage: Official Closure

Saturday, the 16th

Steve called tonight. He told me he and Susan were getting married. October 23. I choked back the tears.

What a surprise to me that I responded like that! I've been hoping they would for a long time. Funny how these things keep catching me off guard.

But at least I'm not afraid to face the feelings head-on now, realizing feeling the pain results in cleaner healing.

Thank you, Lord.

"Because you set the Lord always before you, you shall not be moved."

ven though I knew in my head that Steve was gone, there was still a part of me that wouldn't admit it was really over. As unlikely as it was, there was a sliver of a chance that he would come back. Anything is possible—until the day he actually got remarried. That day the door shut forever.

1. *How do I respond when he tells me he is getting married?*

I wish I could give you the perfect answer. But from my experience, I don't think there was any way I could have prepared a response. Even though it was not news to me that Steve and Susan had been considering marriage, when it became reality, I was stunned.

I vividly recall the night he called to tell me it was official. There was an instant ache in my stomach and my throat burned as I fought back the tears. All I wanted to do was finish the conversation gracefully and be alone. In a flat voice I offered my congratulations and inquired as to the date. (Sometimes left brain facts can temporarily distract the right brain feelings.)

I don't know if he was expecting any particular response from me, and thankfully I didn't have the time or energy to engage in game-playing. It may be an enticing opportunity for some women to make a last-ditch effort to manipulate or lash out at their ex. But remember the goal of making healthy choices.

Ask yourself, "What is best for *me* in this situation?" "Will what I say make him change his mind?" Consider the results of your decision. Will it help heal the relationship or fuel the fire? How will I feel about myself tomorrow? I've had to learn not to allow Steve's words or actions to dictate my responses. This detachment is a process that takes time and practice.

Looking back, I see that I was in the ball park of healthy responses. In fact, I probably could have been even more neutral. It seems like the best response would be a non-emotional acknowledgment that you heard what he said. Period. You do not have to say anything else to him.

But when you are alone, let it rip! Let the feelings out. Cry. Yell! Do whatever you have to as you feel the pain. Maybe for some women, there will only be relief. Whatever you are feeling, be sure to take the healthiest steps in processing them.

2. Why does it feel like I'm starting all over again in working through my feelings?

I thought I was doing pretty well. Life seemed to be progressing, and the painful moments were becoming much less frequent. Part of me was even hoping for this remarriage just for the sake of closure. Knowing there was still a remote chance of reconciliation was both a blessing and a curse. Although the possibility offered hope, the torment of emotional ups and downs was a curse. Trying to go on with my life yet leaving part of my heart open for Steve was a cruel combination. It was almost like losing a loved one to cancer. As long as they're alive there's still hope, yet one wonders if the suffering is worth it. Death brings grief and loss, but also finality and relief from pain. I would still work through my grief, but at least I would be free from keeping the wound open. Final closure would mean eventual healing.

With the progress I had been making, I was discouraged by this apparent setback. When Steve dropped the news, I was suddenly engulfed by all those same painful feelings that I thought were in the past. Not only was I hurting from the feelings themselves, but I felt like a failure. It was as if all the effort and wise choices up to this point were erased, and I had no "back-up file." I told myself I shouldn't be feeling this way. What did I do wrong, and why bother any more if there won't be any lasting results?

I talked with my counselor. His wisdom took a while to sink in, but thankfully it did.

To begin with, we need to let go of any expectations we have about where we "should" be on a healing time line. There is no absolute standard. Instead, the healthiest focus is on making wise choices. Have I been consistent with the survival checklist? (See Chapter 1.) If so, there will be progress. I may not always see it, and it may require one step back for each two steps forward. I felt better being reassured that I was on the right track and my efforts were not wasted.

I was also pleasantly surprised to realize that there *was* a back-up file. After all this time of re-programming myself to feel the feelings and then to work them out in a healthy way, the pattern was beginning to come more naturally.

We are not responsible for our feelings that come uninvited. Nobody will be held accountable for pain or anger or grief. It's what we *do* with these unwelcome intruders that is crucial.

I was beating myself for the feelings that welled up inside of me because I thought they were a sign of weakness and failure. Instead I should have acknowledged and accepted them right away. I didn't have to like them, but they were part of me and there was a reason for them. Then after I felt them (ouch!), I could think about each one, write my feelings, talk about the situation and my responses and cry as much as I wanted.

This was so important for me to understand because life never stops bringing unwanted surprises. God never promised us a pain-free, comfortable life here on this earth. On the contrary, He told us that trials would be the norm, not the exception (John 16:33; 1 Peter 4:12).

When we know the Lord, cling to His promises and use our back-up system to process our feelings, each experience makes us a little stronger and a little more beautiful.

3. What is the best thing for me to be doing on the day of the wedding?

The day our divorce was final, I had purposely made plans to distract myself from thinking about it all day. With Steve's remarriage approaching, I once again faced the question: Should I plan distracting activities or should I face my feelings head-on? I wondered if having deliberate plans was a form of denial. Would it be healthier to arrange to work through my feelings via an appointment with my counselor or to get away alone with my journal?

After sorting through my options and making a choice, I learned several things. Don't deliberately shut out the pain if it comes. There will probably be moments during the day—even the entire week—when feelings will come and go. The circumstances may permit you to work through them at once. Otherwise, be sure to deal with them consciously as soon as you can.

Don't deliberately feed the feelings. I learned this one the hard way. Wanting to treat myself and also to have a distraction, I rented a video. I thought a nice, warm, fuzzy romance would make me feel better. Unfortunately the movie I chose had a tragic ending. (*Sommersby*—they fall in love and he gets hanged at the end.)

Rather than provide an outlet for my brewing tears, it only intensified my pain and created more tears. If I were to do it over again, I would choose a lighthearted comedy/romance, a la Goldie Hawn.

Do make a point to treat yourself. After thinking about what would make you feel good and feel special, choose a healthy way to treat yourself. It would not have been healthy for me to go on a shopping spree or to my favorite all-you-can-eat restaurant. Consider a massage, new shoes, a long-distance phone call you've been wanting to make, a new plant, dinner out with your friends, a new nightie, a new book or music tape, a new hairstyle or a manicure.

Just because there is one person (your ex) who may not think you are wonderful, you *are* special. God says so, and we have to choose to believe Him.

As you approach this day, anticipating its pain, you can walk through this valley knowing life will go on and you are healing.

4. When I finally feel strong enough to look at his and her rings, how do I respond verbally and emotionally?

As humans, we are well-equipped with a survival technique known as denial. It enables us to block out as untrue or nonexistent things that are just too painful to believe as untrue or nonexistent. Unfortunately, most of us have learned to employ this survival technique as a matter of convenience.

After trying to work through my feelings about Steve's remarriage, I still dreaded seeing their rings. I realized there was part of me that still refused to accept it until I saw his ring and her ring.

I was briefly stunned when I saw them. Denial was no longer an option as painful thoughts flooded me. I had flashbacks of when we had bought our rings fifteen years earlier. I felt anger that *I* was the one that was supposed to be his wife, not her. I felt resentment that her ring was more expensive than mine. I felt confusion at the wrongness of this picture. Finally, I grieved. It's really over.

Although I later went through the steps of working through my feelings, at that moment I was groping for the right words to say. Do I let loose with all the hurtful and angry words just waiting at the tip of my tongue? Do I offer a compliment or congratulations? Or do I say nothing?

I chose the latter. Compliments would have been hypocritical for me, and angry words would have only stirred up trouble. Just saying nothing was my healthiest choice.

They didn't need to know that I noticed the rings, and they certainly didn't need to know my feelings.

Each time I see the rings now, it gets a little easier. I don't know if I'll ever be able to totally accept his remarriage. But I do know that facing the painful truth comes one step at a time.

5. How do I deal with the feelings of worthlessness now that I've been replaced?

The phone book lists them as "Steve and Susan Smith." The child support checks I receive have both of their names at the top. I used to be the "Mrs." of Mr. and Mrs. Smith. Now there is a dif-

ferent Mr. and Mrs. Smith where I am not included or wanted.

I've been plagued by questions. Why did he go
through all that hassle just to settle down again
with someone else? What does she have that I
don't? What did I do wrong? I always come away
with even more questions than answers. I may
never know, and I have to be willing to accept
that.

Part of me is inclined to think maybe he's not
really happy after all and wishes he had stuck
around to work things through. Maybe now that
it's too late, he realizes what a good deal he had
with me. I don't know to what degree this is true,
but sometimes it makes me feel a little better. If I
think about it too long, it makes me sad, because
after all the pain caused by this divorce, he might
not even be happy. So this train of thought for me
is counterproductive.

When I struggle with feelings of worthlessness, I'm learning to focus directly on my value
as a person. Forget Steve. Set aside my failed
marriage. Let go of hurtful childhood memories.
Stop thinking, "If only I were thinner." It's so
easy, especially in our culture today, to allow appearance and circumstance to determine our
worth.

I am not any better or any worse in God's eyes
if I'm married or divorced. God is not impressed
when I've lost a few pounds, nor does He love me
less when I've gained some.

We are all sinners from birth, already alienated

from Him and destined for hell. And in that condition, He loved us and sent His Son to die for us. That the God of the universe, our Creator, was willing to die for us, makes the most incredible statement of our worth. (And all we have to do is believe!)

I get into self-esteem trouble when I place the wrong people or circumstances in a position to dictate my worth. If I allow Steve's rejection to destroy me, that is in essence a slap in God's face. I am attempting to place Steve in a higher position than God Himself, by wanting Steve's acceptance above God's acceptance.

I have been replaced by Susan. It is a fact, and it hurts. But I am learning to accept the hurt and my freedom to feel. I am also learning to separate my self-worth from the actions and words of anyone else. Anyone, that is, except God.

And I could never be replaced by anyone else in God's heart.

Reflection:

1. How can you best respond if and when he tells you he's getting married?

2. When feelings arise and you are discouraged at apparent lack of progress, of what can you remind yourself that will bring encouragement?

3. Plan what you will do for yourself on the day of his wedding.

4. To what extent have you been able to fully accept that he is remarried, and to what extent are you shielding yourself with denial?

5. To whom have you granted the right to determine your worth—society, your ex, the mirror, etc.? Write a positive statement of your worth and read it out loud. (I am a valuable person because _____.)

Chapter 11

Other Men:
Fact and
Fantasy

Monday, the 4th

The flowers Rick gave me are falling apart, all except the daisy. I am reminded that even if (best case scenario) Rick and I do get together, he will get old and die, and I will get old and die. The relationship will have its ups and downs—the only One who will never change is God and His Word.

Twenty years ago in my pre-marriage days, dating was an entirely different scenario. I was young and innocent. My career and childbearing years were still ahead of me. The world awaited my conquest. And Prince Charming would burst into my life at any moment.

Twenty years later, I am approaching middle age. My career is fluctuating. I am no longer idealistic. The world is a mess. My marriage was a failure. And the only thing about to burst into my life is menopause.

I've had to accept that Prince Charming does not—and never will—exist. As I seriously consider the pros and cons of remarriage, I pray that I will proceed carefully and with my eyes wide open. I can keep alive the fantasy of a perfect husband and continue my search in vain. I can resign myself in despair to a lifetime of singleness. Or I can face reality, proceeding one step at a time, as I seek God's best in the next chapter of my life.

1. Will my keen awareness of this void in my life (that is, lack of a man) get better or worse with time?

When Scripture refers to marriage as "becoming one," that's exactly what happens. Whether the marriage was happy or rocky, two people have become one entity. When one of the two is snatched away, the other is left with a tremendous vacuum.

Similar to the laws of the physical universe, this sudden emptiness becomes a sucking force, a black hole that grasps anything to fill the void.

This emptiness alone is enough to drive a recently divorced woman into a premature or unhealthy relationship. But when emptiness is combined with a shattered self-esteem, the odds against refraining from unhealthy relationships are tremendous. Many other factors also play a part in this struggle, including financial needs, sexual needs, pride and retaliation. The wounded former wife may feel a powerful urge to show her ex that she can get someone too.

It took me several months before I realized I was doing this. I was not consciously aware of desperately seeking a man, but there was an unseen force within. I was clutching the Prince Charming dream that someone could take away my pain and make me happy again. And I wanted happiness *now*.

I wondered what was wrong with me. Why was it taking so long? I often fantasized that there were many wonderful men just waiting for a chance to be with me.

What I didn't realize was that each day that passed was a blessing in disguise. I did not know that my real need was time. Time to heal. Time to grow. Time to discover who I was and establish my unique identity. Only then would I be fit to enter a healthy relationship. I needed to be in a place where I was able to give and love, not just to have my void filled.

As the years pass since the divorce, my understanding of what I need becomes clearer. And as my life goes on, the intensity of the initial void has diminished. What was once a painful emptiness which I was desperate to fill has, for the most part, healed.

What I am now prone to experience is a natural longing for healthy, intimate companionship. As it comes and goes, I see it not as a fix to take away the pain Steve caused, but as a normal desire for relational fulfillment.

I don't know if it will become more intense with time, or if I will become more content with my singleness.

I do know that I am free to feel these feelings as they come and to seek the Lord in making healthy choices.

2. What is God's will for me: Should I remain single, or how will I know when I am ready for remarriage?

Many times during the long dark valleys, one of the distant hopes that kept me going was the dream of finding love once again. The devastating realization that my marriage was over was made tolerable only because I had hope for a second chance . . . until . . .

Someone suggested that remarriage may not be an option according to the Bible. At first I laughed it off, categorizing them as fanatic and self-righteous. Then I stumbled across a Bible verse which stopped me (Matthew 5:31-32), a reference which seemed to imply that remarriage was adultery.

At first I tried to explain it away with my own reasoning, until finally I came to the place where I had to be honest. Did I want to know God's truth and choose *His* way, or did I want to close my eyes and choose *my* way?

It was difficult, but after a while I was able to come to the Lord honestly. I told Him what I wanted and that I wanted a nice clear Bible verse giving His permission for me to remarry. And then I begged Him that if that was not His will for me, He would flood me with contentment and with the grace to obey. I also prayed that if He did not want me to remarry, He would "close the doors" and not allow it to happen.

So I began my search. I read books warning against remarriage after divorce and books encouraging it. I talked with pastors and other people, divorced and non-divorced. And I came away with about 743 different opinions.

It was tempting to pick the one I wanted. But deep down I needed to know that between God and me, my choice would have His blessing. I needed the peace resulting from seeking *God's* truth, not man's opinions.

The best way for me to finally arrive at a conclusion was to read Scripture only. Not books, but only the Bible. And then I read commentaries on the divorce/remarriage verses (1 Corinthians 6:16; 1 Corinthians 7; Deuteronomy 24:1-4; Mark 10:1-12; 1 Timothy 4:3; Matthew 1:19; Matthew 19:1-10).

I arrived at what I felt is God's will for my life. I don't feel 100 percent comfortable telling *you* what His will is. But seek Him and His truth, and He will lead you. (I am not a theologian. Because there are many differences of opinion on these issues, I encourage you to search the Scriptures and seek the counsel of your own pastor.)

My conclusions were as follows:

- God's ideal for man and woman is one marriage to last a lifetime (Matthew 19:4-6).

- God hates divorce and all the pain it brings (Malachi 2:16).

- God loves me, regardless of what I have or haven't done (Romans 5:8).

- God's grace through Jesus Christ is bigger than any sin of mine (Romans 3:23-29).

- I want to choose God's very best for my life, even if it differs from my dreams and desires; and as I seek Him, His desires become mine (Psalm 37:4).

- God allows divorce because we are sinners (Matthew 19:8).

- If one partner commits unrepentant adultery, the other is free (Matthew 5:32; Matthew 19:9; 1 Corinthians 7:15).

- Paul encourages those who have the gift of singleness to remain single (1 Corinthians 7).

- God will guide the lives of those who trust Him, fear Him and seek Him (Proverbs 3:5-6; 9:10).

I now have a clear conscience that before God alone, I am free to remarry. Yet I am also willing to remain single, should He want that for me. (*He* will supply the contentment and self-control if I am to remain single, because humanly speaking, it won't come naturally to me.)

If He does want me to marry again, how will I know if I'm ready? (I thought I was ready the first time I married.)

Readiness may differ with each individual, but it seems to be primarily an attitude. Readiness is evidenced by a frame of mind that is waiting to give out of love and to enjoy the pleasures of a healthy, intimate, committed relationship. If I am seeking a man to meet my needs and to fill a void or if I'm just wanting to be married, a red flag goes up. I need to be healthy, stable, confident and content before I am ready to enter into the challenges of a lifelong relationship.

In talking with other single women, I've heard two perspectives. One says, "I just want to be married. I wish Mr. Right would hurry up and come along so I can get on with my life, and then I'll be happy."

The other attitude says, "I realize my life is missing something, but I also know life is not necessarily better on the married side of the fence. I will give thanks for all my blessings and make healthy choices to be the best I can be. If a wonderful, godly man comes into my life and love grows between us, I will be open to marriage. But until then, I will fill my life with good things and not seek any man just to be married."

Not only does this second mind-set show evidence of readiness to remarry, it also provides strength and freedom as you become the beautiful person God has intended.

God gives the gift of singleness one day at a time.

3. Is it OK to look around or flirt?

If your conscience is clear before the Lord regarding a green light for remarriage, then by all means revive your flirting skills. Some may need a refresher course. Others would be qualified to teach the course. Either way, enjoy your new-found freedom with a few cautions.

First, be aware of your own motives. What do you want? If your desires are self-serving and immoral, stop now and rethink your choices. Talk to someone you trust and respect. If you're motivated by feminine playfulness and you just want to enjoy some brief innocent male-female interaction, open up and have a great time. The key is whether the flirting is to be enjoyed as an end in itself or intended as a means to a sexually impure end. Check your motives, and then be sure the man clearly understands.

Second, be tuned to the man's responses and discerning of his motives. He may have his own agenda, or he may incorrectly interpret your playfulness as a come-on. Since I am relatively trusting and naive, this has been an area I've had to work on. I try to back off before the stakes get too high.

This leads to the third caution: Know when the flirting is appropriate and when it is not. There will be some people and some settings where it would be wise to refrain from flirting: where the person is a stranger and you have no reason to believe he is a Christian; in business or work-related settings where others may be offended; where the other person obviously is not interested; where flirting may be interpreted as self-serving when your attention should be focused on something (someone) else; where the man is married—even if you think it might be safe. Use your judgment, and when in doubt, don't. There are a lot more dangerous wackos out there than ever before. (And remember, there will be plenty of other opportunities.)

Fourth, be aware of the power of your hormones. As women, we share many similarities in this area, yet no one knows your body as well as you do. PMS may cause teariness in one person and homicidal tendencies in others. Ovulation may never be noticed in one person but may send another on a super-charged man hunt. (This would be me.)

I was never aware of this until after the divorce, and even then it took me awhile to make a connection between the two. Now I know, and I can prepare myself in advance. Every month, mid-cycle, I turn into this incredible man-magnet, searching for a man. I find myself looking at every single man—on the road, in the stores, anywhere. And the scary part is they all look good! So I've had to learn to be careful what situations I allow myself to be in at this time and not to trust my feelings of attraction toward anyone that week. (It all usually balances out, because two weeks later I don't need men, and I don't want them around.) I've also found it helpful to channel my sexual energy into an enjoyable project of some kind. Not only can it be an effective distraction, but I make good use of the energy and come away with a sense of accomplishment.

The final word of caution as you flirt: Be yourself without overdoing it. Find the balance between relaxing and not needing to be absolutely perfect, and yet not appearing desperate. As you enjoy your freedom to play a little, keep in mind that you are carving out your reputation.

4. When should I start dating again, and where do I find good Christian men?

Depending upon how long you were married and how old you were when you said "I do," a long time may have passed since your dating days.

For me, it seems like so much has changed. The world is different. I have matured. The "fish in the sea" are few and far between. And the rules of dating have changed.

When I began to consider dating again, I just assumed I'd dig out and dust off what I knew from previous experiences. It didn't take long to realize it's an entirely different game and I'd have to learn all over again.

I wondered if I was really ready or if I needed a little more time. Circumstantially everything was in order. The divorce was final, so I was morally free to go out. Unfortunately, I entered into an intense relationship too soon. Looking back, I can see that I needed more time to establish my own identity and work through some issues before I could participate in a healthy, romantic relationship.

What I needed was a good male friend with no sexual attraction on either part. I would not recommend re-entering the dating world until you have experienced complete closure with your ex and are healthy enough to begin another relationship. Once Steve had remarried, I was able to go forward with my life, and by then I had learned and grown.

If I were to chronicle my dating experiences since then, we'd need another book. I've had quite a variety. It has been fun, and each experience has brought growth. With each individual and each date, I've learned a little more about myself and what I need and want.

At first I was eager to attend the largest reputable Christian singles group in the area. I was sure I'd meet my Prince Charming.

What a disappointment. Not only were there no men I was interested in, I got "hit on" by some slick car salesman (who, incidentally, didn't let up until a year later). My mistake: Never give out your business card or your last name, address or phone number.

But I didn't give up. I went to the New Year's Eve Christian singles party, once again certain

I'd meet Prince Charming. No such luck. Out of 400 people, there was no one. And I came home at 9:00, depressed.

Then I thought I'd try the personal ads in the paper. It was always fun to read them, but I never thought I'd be "that desperate." Until the day I found Mr. Right: Christian, my age, loves children, attractive, loves to be active and also to cuddle by the fire.

Too good to be true! So I called and left a message about myself. (This three-minute call cost me $11.) He returned my call a week later, and then I realized he wasn't too good. Thankfully, I was able to see the red flags and say, "No, thank you."

So I learned not to trust the ads. I still read them for fun, but I'm a little wiser now. When I see one that looks ideal, I mentally add a few lines to it: self-centered, lazy, been with many women, snores, tends to get into debt. . . . Just a reality check.

On the other hand, if *I* were to place an ad about myself, I'd have men lining up at my front door. Or so I thought. After four months of my "perfect" ad in a national Christian singles paper, I was back at square one. Plenty of responses (including one from what appeared to be a serial killer), but none of them were my idea of Prince Charming. So at least I can say, "Been there, done that." It was fun and a good learning process, but the fantasy didn't come true.

I continued my quest for the perfect place to

meet my perfect man. I struck out at church, although I still keep my eyes open for visitors. The
best times for grocery shopping are after 5 o'clock
on weekdays or anytime Saturday. Saturdays are
also the best at the golf course. (You don't have to
play, just go and look.) The guys at the health
club, for the most part, seem to be preoccupied
with their own muscles and are on a flesh hunt
themselves. Also, I have found that not many single fathers attend school programs. I still keep my
eyes open at work, but so far that hasn't been a
productive source of eligible men.

You might be laughing and shaking your head
at my efforts. But I needed to know that I tried all
these places and I'm not missing anything. Some
of you knew that a long time ago without having
to go through the disappointments and unfulfilled
expectations that I did.

I am now at the point where I am more relaxed.
I will probably always keep at least half an eye
open for eligible men because I enjoy that. But
I'm learning to go on with my life and do the
things I want to do without holding my breath for
Mr. Right.

I have gone to some Christian singles activities
expecting only to have fun. And I came away feeling good.

As time passes, the opportunities to meet people
will increase. Just in the last year, I've been intro-
duced to four wonderful Christian men by people
I already knew. I didn't have to do a thing. They
came to me right where I was. (They're all in the

just-a-good-friend category right now, but that's OK too.)

As you continue your regular activities, you will eventually meet someone there. A good friend pointed out that this is an ideal way to meet others. You will already have something in common, and you are not having to deviate from your lifestyle to do so. Just be yourself, be a lady and don't worry about the "rules." Either he'll let you know the rules or you can make them up together.

In the long run, my future is in God's hands. I can burn up energy looking, or I can wait patiently. (Or I can sneak a peek while I wait patiently.) The best attitude for me is to trust Him while participating in activities and to enjoy meeting Christian single men while placing my expectations and dreams on the promises of God.

5. How can I keep my hopes and expectations realistic so I don't get hurt again?

Years ago, a man named Edward Mote wrote these words: "My hope is built on nothing less than Jesus' blood and righteousness. I dare not trust the sweetest frame, but wholly lean on Jesus' name."

He is our hope, and we dare not lean on anything or anyone else. What an encouraging and admirable daily goal. Why do we put our hopes in people and other things? Whenever I put my hope in the Lord, without fail I eventually find peace and fulfilled promises. Whenever I put my hope in people, I find disappointment and shattered dreams.

When Rick came along after the divorce, I thought he was it. I had known him for many years and had always admired him. My wildest dream came true as he swept me off my feet in a whirlwind romance. We talked seriously about marriage and declared our mutual love.

But when he walked out of my life, I came crashing down almost as if it were another divorce. And I couldn't tell anyone because they were still extending their sympathies to me about Steve.

Rick came in and out of my life for the next three years. And as my other dates came and went, the deepest part of my heart was reserved for him. Although I tried not to feed the dreams, there was always hope. Until I recently heard he was getting married soon.

It was time to let go. And it hurt terribly. My hopes were worthless, and I have had to learn to live with all the memories and "what ifs."

There have been two other men I thought were going to be it, but the Lord also closed the door on those relationships. I am trying to learn from these experiences, not only to lessen the unnecessary pain of future disappointments, but also to grow.

One thing I'm learning is to guard my heart and not be so quick to open it up. As I approach a new relationship, I try to make a conscious choice about allowing myself to be in the position where I could get hurt again. If I decide it's worth the risk, I will become vulnerable. Then I am also willing to feel the pain of rejection. It may sound a little cynical, but I'm actually starting to get pretty good at processing the pain of rejection. At least I know now that I will survive and life will go on. I will be stronger and wiser because of it.

I am also learning to focus on only the Lord to meet my needs. My highest and deepest hope should be in Him, the only One in this universe who can always be trusted. The only One in this universe who truly wants the best for me.

To stay focused, I have to constantly keep His Word in my mind. Notes and verses I put on the refrigerator have been a real encouragement. I've found three passages to be especially helpful.

- *Psalm 62*—The whole chapter is good, but I like verses five and six: "Find rest, O my soul, in God alone; / my hope comes from him. / He alone is my rock and my salvation, / ... I will not be shaken."

  I need to place all my expectations in Him, and I won't be disappointed or shaken when circumstances don't go the way I want.

- *Psalm 84:11-12* "No good thing does he withhold / from those whose walk is blameless. / O LORD Almighty, / blessed is the man who trusts in you."

  As my walk is in line with His will, I can

count on Him to meet my needs. If He with-
holds something that I wanted, then I must
believe that it was not good (His best) for me.
He has something better.

- *Jeremiah 17:5-8* "Cursed is the one who trusts
  in man, / . . . He will be like a bush in the
  wastelands; / . . . blessed is the man who
  trusts in the LORD, / whose confidence is in
  him. / He will be like a tree planted by the
  water / . . . It does not fear when heat
  comes; / . . . and never fails to bear fruit."

  When I allow myself to put my hopes in
  any person, I will be disappointed. People
  fail. But when I put my dreams and desires
  on the Lord and His plan for me, I will flour-
  ish. He can always be trusted. I will feel the
  slap of a relational closed door because I am
  willing to be vulnerable. Yet I am trying to
  place my highest hopes in the Lord, realizing
  that here on earth fallen humanity is the best
  I'm going to get.

The Lord is our Prince Charming, but we have
to wait to fully experience that bliss. In the meantime, I know there's no man, no matter how wonderful, who can ever meet all my needs. As I seek
God and His best, I will be able to keep a balanced perspective.

*6. What is the best response to the pressures of well-
meaning family and friends?*

Everybody has an opinion. Everybody has an opinion about your life. And yet not one of them has ever lived your life.

Over the years, hopefully we learn who dispenses wisdom, and we learn to seek them out. Unfortunately, as we receive unsolicited advice from others it is not always easy to discern the wisdom from the meddling.

"You're still young. You'll find someone."

"Honey, you deserve a good man."

"You shouldn't be rushing into anything this soon."

"Just be careful."

Have you received comments like these? And just what help were each of these supposed to provide? The first two were probably intended to be an encouragement, but implied that my ultimate goal was to be married and that if I wasn't, there was something wrong. They also suggested that my worth as a person was reflected in having a good man. The last two indicated a fear or insecurity on the part of the advisor and failed to include anything positive that I could use.

I'm learning to listen politely to people's comments and acknowledge that I heard them. Whether or not I take steps to implement the advice is my choice. I have to honestly examine both the comment and its source and then be willing to heed any truth I find.

Praying for wisdom as well as talking with my close friends and family always helps me in the validation process.

Don't be surprised when people offer advice, and don't let it fluster you. Be willing to seek and recognize the beneficial words, and let the rest roll off your back. (You may even find some of it amusing!)

7. What guidelines will be most helpful as I attempt to set standards for what I want in a husband?

As a potential recycled wife (not used, but recycled), I fluctuate from second-chance optimism to distrusting pessimism. Part of me desperately wants to find that wonderful man with whom I can finally have a fulfilling marriage. And part of me is so gun-shy I wonder if I'll ever be able to trust a man again. I also wonder if I'll ever be able to trust my own judgment again.

At first I found I was very attracted to men who possessed the qualities that Steve lacked. I noticed that I was willing to overlook some blatant faults because I was so impressed with the areas of strength I had wanted to see in Steve. I realized this pendulum effect was not necessarily healthy. Every man will have strengths and weaknesses. It is my responsibility to choose what I am and am not willing to live with.

When I was dating Steve, I had a list of about twenty things I wanted in a husband. (I had to learn to flex a little.) This time around I've boiled it down to three absolute essentials, and the rest are on the wish list. In screening potential marriage partners, these three requirements are non-negotiable:

- must be a Christian who is growing and walking with the Lord
- must be attractive (to me)
- must have a healthy relationship with Danny

Unless these three characteristics are present, I will not pursue the relationship. If these three are met, I have several things I think are important and several things I'd love to have. Over time the list may change. But thinking through these values has been a good exercise for me. Here's my wish list:

- should be committed to his physical health
- should be financially stable
- should be above average intelligence
- would like him to like animals
- would like him to be musical
- would like him to agree with my political views

I encourage you to sort through your priorities as I did. Choose the top, nonnegotiable essentials and make an accountability commitment with someone. Then think through the variables, deciding what you can afford to give up. Once you are hopelessly in love, it will be almost impossible to establish your standards. And never, never assume he will change.

Finally, identify your top four to six needs and be able to communicate those to your prospective husband. These are areas where you *need* your husband to show his love for you. Without them, the marriage may be in trouble. Can he make a reasonable effort to meet those needs?

I have identified six things that are essential for my husband to do to demonstrate his love to me:

- be a spiritual leader (pray together, talk openly about things of the Lord, help me grow)

- express affection (nonsexual, such as back rubs, hugging and holding, looking in my eyes and telling me how special I am)

- take care of himself physically (eat healthy and exercise, keep attractive appearance)

- build me up and let me feel special (let me know I am number one in his life, make decisions together, be romantic)

- support my commitment to health and fitness (encourage me to get enough sleep, protect my priority for healthy eating and exercise, give me time alone)

- play (have fun, laugh together, let me be silly)

I want to be respected for my high standards yet remain reasonable enough to allow room for a growing, fallible human being. I hope my potential future husband will do the same.

Reflection:

1. How strong is your sense of urgency to fill the void left by your ex-husband? Is there some-

one you can share this with who will be by your side to help you keep perspective?

2. Have you come before the Lord with an open heart, seeking His will for your future? On what basis can you honestly say you are free (or not free) to remarry?

3. List the men in your "fair game"—healthy flirting—category, and make another list of those who are off-limits.

4. Where is the best place for *you* to meet quality Christian men? What places should you avoid?

5. Evaluate your expectations: Are you placing them in one man or in God? Where will these expectations take you in ten or twenty years?

6. Who can you count on for wise input for your life?

7. What are your nonnegotiable standards for a future husband? What are your five strongest needs for him to meet?

Chapter 12

The Harvest:
All Things
Work
Together
for Good

Wednesday, the 13th

Oh Lord, what a mess!

Do You think You can actually pull a Romans 8:28 out of this?

We'll see.

"All things work together for good to those who love God, to those who are the called according to His purpose" (Romans 8:28, NKJV). This warm fuzzy verse is one we all love to claim. But when you're in the bottom of a pit, promises that strong seem impossible.

I questioned that verse when I was overcome in the pit of divorce. Now I can testify, as thousands have over the years, that God keeps His word. When we are His children and we love Him, He is capable of causing *everything* (including the pain) to effectively contribute to His ultimate purpose and our ultimate good. He will be glorified, and we will become the beautiful people He intends us to be.

Who would have thought so much good could come from so much agony! Here's what I have gained.

1. Humility—new empathy with divorced people

I've been humbled by this eye-opening divorce experience. I've learned I am in no position to judge anyone else. I always felt a little self-righteous about the good job I was doing as a wife. I assumed anyone who had succumbed to divorce just didn't try hard enough. Or perhaps they made poor choices along the way. I classified them in a sort of stained-for-life failure category.

I never doubted that God's grace was broad enough to include everyone. It's just that I knew if

I were that person, *I* would have done it differently.

Well, here I am. I *am* that person. And I didn't do it differently. Thank God that His grace is greater than I ever imagined, it can include me. And it can include *anyone* I start to condemn. Anyone.

Now that I've been divorced, on occasion I'll feel the sting of scorn from the self-righteous non-divorced. I try to remember not to condemn them, because I was there not too long ago.

2. Deeper understanding of the reality of Scripture

I always believed the Bible, but I never needed God's promises as desperately as I did in the throes of divorce.

All the verses I had memorized and read through the years suddenly took on full-color, three-dimensional meaning. Passages I had flatly read many, many times were now leaping out at me as if for the first time.

Prior to my divorce, God and His Word were like a commodity to be used for eternal life after death and during times of grief. My life was so comfortable I was not aware of how much I desperately needed Him.

When I was stripped of all of the comforts and securities of life, I could turn only to God. Because I had never cried out to Him from the depths of my being, clinging to Him for survival, I had never experienced the reality of His promises.

My need gave me the opportunity to see God's faithfulness. I soaked up Scripture, not in great quantities, but with great frequency. I needed to be reminded all through the day that "the eternal God is your refuge, and underneath are the everlasting arms" (Deuteronomy 33:27). Comfort.

I needed the energy that came from being reminded that "those who hope in the LORD will renew their strength. . . . They will run and not grow weary, they will walk and not be faint" (Isaiah 40:31). Strength.

I needed to know this pain was only temporary and something beyond my comprehension was yet to come. "In this you greatly rejoice, though now for a little while you may have had to suffer grief in all kinds of trials. These have come so that your faith . . . may be proved genuine and may result in praise, glory and honor when Jesus Christ is revealed. . . . Though you do not see him now, you believe in him and are filled with an inexpressible and glorious joy" (1 Peter 1:6-8). Hope.

And I continue to read and learn and seek daily application of His Word. I will never doubt His promises. And I will never take them for granted.

3. Greater faith and a closer walk with God

He's always been there, even before I was conceived. But I was never so keenly aware of His presence as I was in the dark valley of divorce. He held me up. He gave me a focus. He brought me through. And as I look back, I can testify that I wouldn't be where I am today without the Lord.

As I look ahead to the tomorrows and the unknown valleys yet to come, I can trust. He is the same God He has been since before time. He is the same God that sent His Son Jesus Christ to die for my sin. He is the same God who carried me through the valley. And He is the same God who will work for my good and His glory tomorrow.

I'm learning to respect and to trust His sovereignty. I have no doubt that He loves me, but I've often questioned if He was doing the right thing. Sometimes I've even used prayer time to offer suggestions.

Now after almost forty years of life, I'm beginning to consider that maybe God—almighty, all-knowing God—just might know something I don't. Lots of things. Everything!

I'm so thankful that He didn't actually do the things I wanted, the things I thought were best at the time. And I will choose to trust Him again and again when He allows pain in my life or says no to what I want.

He knows something I don't, and He loves me too much not to give me His very best.

4. Sharper eternal perspective; to loosely hold false securities of this life

When Steve left, I had no husband (no companion, no provider). My health deteriorated (no physical security). I went into debt (no financial security). The U.S. was at war in the Persian Gulf, and I was plagued with fear of terrorism or all-out war (no faith in my country). I might lose my house (no home). And Steve had filed for custody of Danny (no child?!). There wasn't much left.

I would not consider it fair to compare my situation with Job in the Bible. You may not consider it fair to compare my situation with yours, but we all share a common choice: When we are stripped of our earthly comforts and securities, we can either turn bitter and continue to seek temporal things to fill the emptiness, or we can fall helplessly into the arms of God.

Psalm 62 has been a real encouragement to me as a reminder to place my hope in nothing and nobody except God. Nothing and no person in this life can be depended on 100 percent. We will be disappointed unless we transfer our securities to our Creator and Redeemer.

Hebrews 12:1-2 reminds us to lay aside all of the things that distract us and to put all of our hopes and efforts in Jesus Christ alone. The joy and satisfaction to come cannot be imagined.

Everything we see will sooner or later be dead or destroyed. Everything. It's the One we can't see and the value of the intangible qualities such as love, faith and obedience that will last forever (2 Corinthians 4:16-18).

I can enjoy pleasures here and live my life prudently, but I remember that there are no guarantees in this life. Tomorrow it may all suddenly be gone.

As long as I am walking with God and have my hope securely in Him, I will be OK.

It won't be long until we'll be with Him in heaven. Forever safe. Forever satisfied. Forever OK.

5. Personal character development

One of my favorite "refrigerator" verses which I looked at daily was Jeremiah 17:7-8. The passage contrasts the person who trusts in *man* and withers up with the person who trusts in *God* and flourishes. Because their roots go deep into the Source, those who trust in God continue to bear fruit regardless of the storms or droughts.

Looking back, I see that even in pain I was able to bear fruit. Sometimes more. Sometimes less.

People commented to me that my faith in God and faithfulness to Him were an inspiration to them. I didn't feel like I was inspiring anyone; I was busy just surviving. But the encouragement that I was doing more than just surviving helped me to focus on the positive: God was using me to touch others.

Galatians 5:22-23 lists the fruit of God's Spirit: love, joy, peace, patience, kindness, goodness, faithfulness, gentleness and self-control. When those beautiful fruits appear in my life, I can thank only God because He is the Source.

I've also grown in emotional strength and self-confidence. I have learned so much and have been stretched beyond what I thought I could bear.

But these painful experiences have blossomed into the blessing of being a survivor—a healthy survivor who is continuing to be the best she can be.

6. Increased knowledge and skills in practical areas (car maintenance, finances, etc.)

One of the things that has been key to my progress in this area is a willingness to learn. At first I was angry and resentful that I should even have to be hanging window shades, assembling vacuum cleaners and attempting to repair toys.

But viewing each project as a challenge has boosted my knowledge, skill and self-esteem. Greater responsibility has resulted in greater accomplishments.

I hope to continue learning for the rest of my life.

7. The ability to minister to others in pain

How often have I heard someone say, "I know how you feel," yet I shut them out because they have never been in my shoes. They just *think* they know how I feel.

Now I can actually say to another woman experiencing divorce, "I've been there. I know a lot of what you're going through. And I will be praying

for you. Give me a call if you ever want to talk."
And then I give her a big hug.

Second Corinthians 1:3-4 points out that one of
the values of our trials is that after we have come
through them ourselves, we can comfort and encourage others who are going through pain.

That is the main reason I've written this book. I
want to pass on to you what I've learned in the
hopes that you will draw comfort and encouragement to help carry you through.

8. Courage to face pain

Psalm 46:1-2 has kept me going many times:
"God is our refuge and strength, an abundantly
available help in trouble. Therefore we will not
fear. . ." (NKJV). The chapter goes on to list some
frightening tragedies, the shattering of things we
depend on in this life.

It's a little like childbirth. Once a woman has
experienced the pain of giving birth, all other dis-
comforts are insignificant. Having endured childbirth pain, I feel confident that I can put up with
anything.

The more we experience the trials and traumas
of life, particularly divorce, the more we are
equipped for what tomorrow may bring.

Romans 8:18-25 is a powerful passage that
speaks of pain and hope. We have to experience
pain to appreciate hope. In the absence of pain,
hope is meaningless. Feeling pain allows me to feel
hope.

When I seek God as my refuge in times of fear, disappointment and pain, my feelings are overcome by hope.

George Matheson writes, "O my God, teach me, when the shadows have gathered, that I am only in a tunnel. It is enough for me to know that it will be all right some day"

9. Knowledge that I have more to learn

Life is a process. Today is tomorrow's yesterday. I'm older now than I've ever been, but younger than I'll ever be. I don't know what tomorrow holds, but I know what I'm supposed to do. As I walk with Him and seek His ways, He will guide and He will bless.

I hope to continue to be used by Him, and to be a channel of comfort and encouragement to others.

I am no longer a wife, but that has not stopped God from continuing His work in my life. And I pray that He will never stop.

I don't know what tomorrow holds, but I know Who holds tomorrow.

I hope you do too.

Reflection:

Start a list of each good thing you have seen come so far from the divorce. Revisit the list every six months, and give thanks that God does keep His promises.

Saturday, the 7th

I did it! I survived dipping back into my journals and finding appropriate parts of it to share. Getting so close to all the pain was hard.

Thank you, Lord, for the healing and the growth, and that You are the same Lord holding me now who held me all the way through.

Exodus 15:26—"I am the Lord, who heals you."

Appendices

A. Other Ex-Wives Share

B. You: A Single Parent

C. Scripture to Consider

D. A Bear with a Badge

Appendix A

Other Ex-Wives Share

The following excerpts contain words of encouragement and advice from other divorced women, most of whom have had time to heal. I asked them to pass on words of wisdom that they felt would have been helpful to them at the time they were where you are now.

"The days will have difficulties ahead, but God loves you. Imagine walking down a path. Each day God has a 'candy basket' to give you. Some days the basket will be obvious, other days it will be off the path and you'll have to search. But there are special things just for you from God. They may be large or small, but there's something good for you every day. Read Jeremiah 29:11."—Annie

"Someone told me it takes three years to get over a divorce. I clung to this because it was a tangible hope. The truth is that in some ways three years is too long and in others it's not enough."—Chris

"I want to affirm you as a person. Allow your-self time to heal from your broken oneness."—Judy

"There is a healing in crying. Give yourself per-mission to cry, then cry until your tears are spent.

"If you don't feel safe crying at home lest some-one hear, try something that worked for me. There was a cemetery close to where I lived. I drove back to a corner and parked under a tree where I was less likely to encounter anyone. Then I rolled up my windows and just let go. There is a respect for privacy in such a place. Mourning is appropriate and accepted, even mourning the death of a marriage."—Brenda

"Don't be hasty. You're hurt and angry which makes it easy to say and do things you will later regret.

"Don't say bad things about their father to or around the kids. They have and need a relation-ship with both of you. My ex-husband and I agreed not to let the kids play us against each other, especially for things. It's easier to stop 'one-upping' each other if you don't start. But it's OK to have different rules at each house."—Janice

"When my home was torn apart by divorce, I was faced with the challenge of restructuring my identity. I was still a mother, but I now played this role as a single parent rather than in tandem. I suddenly became a single person dealing with the world. My identity was no longer tied to the person to whom I had been married. What he did for a living, how he interacted with the world and his opinions no longer touched me, except as they affected our son.

"Becoming my own person and establishing who I am has been, and continues to be, one of my greatest challenges. Eight years after my second divorce, I am still in the process of defining me. Having been twice divorced, I have learned this second time around what I failed to learn the first time.

"Remarrying within two years of my first divorce, I had failed to address the issues of who I am and the nature of my dependency needs. This time, I am taking the time to work on these issues because I have learned by experience that the cost is too high when I fail to examine and nurture myself. What I am becoming and what I continue to be are dependent on this self-knowledge and self-examination."—Jeanine

"I'm thankful I never did speak unkindly of my ex-husband to his parents and family (even after the divorce). They are one blood, and it would not be to anyone's advantage to come between them."—Michelle

"Let yourself feel the pain and allow yourself the freedom to be sick. You would not think of continuing your daily routine as though nothing were wrong if you had surgery or a physical ill-

ness which your doctor said required bed rest and
time off. Then why do you think you need to put
on a brave front and pretend as though nothing is
wrong when you find yourself single again? The
pain of rejection and the pain of a broken heart
due to the separation of your covenant mate need
time for therapy and healing every bit as much as
physical illness.

"You need to be able to share your deepest
thoughts and pain with someone you can trust,
with someone who will listen quietly. Let that
someone hug you, cry with you and feel your
pain. God, through His Son Jesus Christ, truly
understands, but He has placed us here on this
earth to come alongside our sisters and be that listener, to hug, to cry.

"Allow yourself the freedom to experience the
anger, the denial, the acceptance and finally the re-
newal that comes when the natural process of grief
occurs. Don't rush the process, but allow yourself
time. It may take you only a brief time, or it may
take years. There is no magic formula, but trust
God to see you through the process."—Jennifer

"I think two good choices for me were first,
moving—it gave me a new start in a place without
memories where I was free to start some new traditions—and second, taking my last name back—
this helped me figure out who I was and not feel
so lost. After a period of time, I realized it was OK
for me to do this, and it really didn't matter to all
'those' people out there anyway.

"The most emotionally freeing thing for me was realizing (over time) that in this relationship with my ex, whatever I did would not be good enough—according to him. Through the help of a counselor and good friends, I finally realized I had done my best, and everything was not my fault."—Charlotte

"Proverbs 3:5-6 became real. God will provide for His children. Then I learned Second Chronicles 20:12: 'I do not know what to do, but I'm looking at you' (my paraphrase).

"At first there were so many overwhelming things I didn't know what to do. I would throw up my hands and cry out to the Lord, 'I don't know what to do, but You do.' No matter what the circumstances, keep looking up to Him."—Cindy

"Seek godly and family advice from those able to objectively help you. Unfortunately, I acted on unhealthy advice to keep the 'relationship' with my ex and not cause friction over material possessions. I wish I had sought someone who would have looked out for my interests, as I refused alimony and 'gave away the store.' I was not thinking objectively about my needs and my future."—Danielle

"If you have longtime, trusted, wise friends, let them help you make decisions—especially if you're numb. There are usually so many decisions that need immediate attention during and following a divorce. The decisions themselves can be overwhelming. You need not be alone in this. Let them help you. You'll be less likely to regret things later."—Andrea

"Two steps I made immediately were to close our mutual bank accounts and open one in my name only. Although I doubted my husband would leave me penniless, I had to take care of myself. He was the one who forced my hand. I also called a locksmith and had the locks changed on the house. He was surprised, but it forced him to take me seriously."—Lisa

"In the absence of their father, my kids have benefited from playing a sport every year. This has given them needed contact with men (good role models), helped them relate with men and developed skills they feel good about."—Barb

"The most important thing an ex-wife can do is to forgive her ex-spouse. She needs to do it for herself, her kids and for her relationship with the Lord. She need not confuse forgiveness with acceptance, trust or restoration.

"I think forgiveness means that you allow the relationship with your ex-spouse to be as pleasant as possible and relinquish your 'right' to change him or make him feel bad for hurting you. I also think it means praying that the Lord will finish whatever work He has started in the life of that ex-spouse. This is so important to remember if you have children.

"Conflict and bitterness never make children feel safe. They need an atmosphere of peace. It is important for children to know that when the two people they love most in the world are around each other, they will all get along.

"Last year I arranged to meet my ex-husband in California at his parents' house to celebrate our daughter's birthday. On the way down, I asked my little five-year-old if she was looking forward to seeing her dad. (She hadn't seen him in six months.)

"She was a bit hesitant and said, 'But what if you and Daddy don't get along?'

"I assured her that I wasn't going to let anything spoil her special day. Her attitude changed. She was 100 percent enthusiastic. I think it was the best birthday present I could give her, that sense that everything was going to be OK."—Lila

"When you're angry at God, don't keep it inside. Tell Him about it. The Lord says in Psalm 145:18, 'The LORD is near to all who call on him, to all who call on him in *truth*' (emphasis added). He desires your honesty."—Wendy

"Forgiveness makes such a difference in your relationship with the Lord. Sometimes I feel like my divorce is a great big black blotch on my life. I know that the Lord has forgiven me, and I have forgiven myself. But the scars remain. Divorce went against all that I believe, and it was the most excruciating choice I ever made. I need to keep the

channels of communication between me and the
Lord wide open. Forgiveness does that. I don't
want there to be any area that is off limits from
His continued work in me. Holding a grudge or
carrying around bitterness makes an area off limits
to the Lord. I don't ever want to shut Him out, no
matter what it is I need to let go of."—Natalie

"After the initial shock, the total disorientation
of my life and the full force of pain hit me, my
most constant and overwhelming fear was:
'What's going to happen to my kids? How is all
this going to affect them?'

"From those early frightening years to the acceptance of my single parent role and into remarriage and the blended family situation, I have
learned that single parenting can be a wonderful
adventure in learning to trust a loving heavenly
Father.

"I clung to some verses for dear life. My favorite
is Jeremiah 29:11: 'For I know the plans I have for
you,' declares the LORD, 'plans to prosper you and
not to harm you, plans to give you hope and a future.' It was hope I needed most desperately.
Would life ever be fun again?

"I also claimed Philippians 4:13, 19 and Isaiah
54:4. I prayed about everything—large and small.
I used common sense, but I also learned to trust
God when things didn't make sense. He protected
my children and me, and somehow we survived."—Becky

"A big area that I would caution a newly divorced woman in is vulnerability. Divorce is such a big emotional wound. If we could see the wound like we see physical hurts, we would be so cautious. When I was divorced, I felt like I'd had an amputation. Wounds that bad bleed all over the place. We bleed over others emotionally. We may tend to tell people who are not trustworthy about our painful experiences and build relationships with people who will take advantage of our vulnerability. We don't see how bad they are for us until we start to get healthy.

"This is especially true in the area of male-female relationships. Some 'nice' man may come along who 'only wants to be our friend.' Newly divorced people really don't see clearly in this area. It is hard enough to see straight when we are doing great, but add the emotional needs of a broken person, and I think the situation can lead to disaster. The more I felt I needed a man in my life, the less I really should have someone in my life.

"As a newly divorced person, I have to learn all over how to develop friendships with men. Someday someone really special may come along, but then again maybe he won't. Whatever happens, the Lord can make us content.

"Contentment is a daily thing. He is always working it out in me. Some days I feel great. I am glad for my independence. I love being able to go where I want, when I want and spend what I want (I'm reasonable). Then I can come home and fix hot dogs for dinner and work in the yard until it is dark. I don't have to worry about taking care of a spouse or making someone angry about the way I cut the grass.

"But I also struggle with loneliness. I remember one night I went in to check on my daughter. She was asleep and the radio by her bedside was playing a soft sweet song. I looked down at her with her hair spread across the pillow and felt an overwhelming sense of thankfulness to the Lord for sending me such a wonderful child. Along with that, there was a severe twinge of sorrow. I really wished that I had been able to reach out and hold the hand of the one the Lord had meant me to share that moment with. I spent the next fifteen minutes convincing myself and the Lord that I really didn't feel that way.

"Only the Lord can fill us with contentment. And it isn't an always-feel-that-way thing. It comes and goes. But as the Lord reweaves the shredded places of my life, I have more 'content' days than 'discontent' days."—Pamela

"Should you remarry, have God as a vital part of your marriage, have accountable fellowship with other believers as a couple and be transparent with family, seeking wisdom and godly input that they may offer."—Kari

"I praise God that though it has taken four very long years, I am today a whole woman who truly knows that God loves her and that He is her husband and her father. I have learned to be content and am seeing new doors of service and ministry open that I never dreamed possible. Allow yourself the privilege of knowing that you are a woman in whom God is well pleased."—Melissa

"Being single has given me an opportunity to build my self-esteem and rely on God's guidance for my decisions in life. I am much more willing to listen to what God is telling me than I was before."—Carol

"My life has changed radically since my divorce six years ago. I am remarried, in the process of adopting two children, and my heart is right with God. He has used me in ways I would never have been able to be used if it were not for the heartbreak I experienced through divorce."—Robin

"Being single was not my choice, but because of my single status, God has been able to use me in ways He never would have if I were married. I feel that I will not be single forever, but if I am, I know that it will be because God has greater plans for me than I ever would have chosen myself."—Kate

"The impact of my divorce was the most devastating experience I have ever endured.

"My husband and I were in Christian ministry for twenty years, and I had leaned on him and drawn my strength from him. In many ways, he was my god. Due to my poor self-image and the shock of this loss, I pulled away from support and love of people around me when we parted. There were many times when I contemplated suicide, and the only thread that kept me going was knowing that my sons needed their mother.

"Three years passed after our divorce before I could even begin the journey to healing. As I look back at our relationship, I can see how co-dependent and unhealthy our marriage had been. At the age of forty, I took my first college class and seven years later I finally received my degree in human development. The most exciting thing that I have discovered is *me*. I kept my eyes on the Lord for inner healing and found I was a person of worth and value. The Lord *finally* became my personal Savior and friend. Even though I am happily remarried, I know that my joy comes from within, not from any one person.

"I could throw stones at my ex-husband and blame him for all the pain and suffering. However, I also discovered how the *two of us* contributed to an unhealthy relationship. The point at which I became willing to accept my part in the breakdown of our marriage was the beginning of the healing for me. I believe the greatest gift I can give my sons is for them to have a healthy, happy and godly mother. God is in the business of restoration, and when God does the healing, He does good work!"—Evelyn

Appendix B

You: A Single Parent

ormerly a wife and mother, now suddenly a single parent. My immediate
goal is to survive, and to do my best to
help my children through this difficult time.

Each child involved in a broken family experiences pain. The forms in which this pain is mani-
fested externally varies from child to child. For
some, it may be silence, fearfulness, sullenness or
withdrawal. Others may act out in anger, rebellion or hostility. Still others may cry, hurt themselves or resume bed-wetting. Danny became
hostile, lashing out physically and issuing death
threats. He cried in the middle of every night for
over a year, and he experienced panic attacks and
irrational crying at school.

As mothers, now single parents, our responses
to our children may also vary. The crushing load
of our own pain, coupled with the distractions of
the divorce and overwhelming responsibilities,

may obscure our vision. It's possible to become temporarily blind to the needs of our children.

We may be so wounded ourselves that we are too emotionally crippled to bear the additional emotional burden of our children. Since we can see their pain but feel helpless to do anything about it, our own burden is often compounded by guilty feelings because we cannot lessen or stop their hurt.

The following words of wisdom have been helpful to me in endeavoring to meet my son's needs while surviving and becoming stronger myself.

- Reassure them you are not leaving. You love him/her, and you will *never* leave.

- Talk to them about feelings. Reassure them that it's OK to feel these awful things and think these awful thoughts. Then show them appropriate ways to vent the feelings: pillow fights, one minute of screaming, shutting the bedroom door and yelling as loudly as possible, drawing pictures, role playing with puppets or running as fast possible.

- Provide plenty of opportunities for physical activity.

- Buy them an age-appropriate tape of upbeat or soothing Christian music.

- Find out times when a local Christian radio station broadcasts children's or family programs. Listen together.

- Consider taking them to a professional counselor, either for private sessions or family sessions.

- Reassure them it was not their fault that Daddy is gone.

- Take the necessary steps to meet your survival needs. (See the survival checklist in Chapter 1.)

- Ask for help. Locate friends and family who can help out when you need a break or a shoulder to lean on.

- Be sure to encourage their regular activities, friendships and social life.

- As much as possible, maintain or re-establish a consistent routine; they are desperate for stability and security.

- Never bad-mouth their father. It only hurts the children and will ultimately cause resentment against you.

- Unless there is abuse, encourage consistent visitation. He is their father, and as much as *you* may hate him, *they* need him.

- In the absence of their father, seek a godly man to become part of their lives (role model, friend, someone not romantically involved with you).

- Protect the children from witnessing any more arguments. Be cordial to their father when they are listening. If conflict is unavoidable, take care of your business when they are not around.

- In most cases, it's wise to encourage continued contact with *both* sets of grandparents.

- Inform their teachers about your situation, and maintain consistent two-way communication.

- Allow and affirm their childhood. Do not let them grow up too soon by feeling they have to fill the role vacated by their father.

- Read verses that remind them of the love and care promised by our heavenly Father.

- If you can, try to set aside a little time each day just to give them your full attention: play with them or talk or listen. No agenda. Nothing that needs to be done. Just a time when you can enjoy each other.

- Don't try to be supermom. Shoot for the bare minimum, meeting your child's four basic needs: physical, emotional, spiritual, social.

- Consider making a commitment to remain unmarried until your children have reached age eighteen. They desperately need your time and emotional energy. You will look back and have no regrets about not being there for them 100 percent. Your stress level will be much better without the added confusion of new relationships, step-children, other ex-wives, etc.

- Remember that nobody on earth could be a better mother to your children than you, and God loves them even more than you ever will.

Appendix C

Scriptures to Consider

$\mathcal{I}$ have been collecting the verses on the following pages over the past few years and have grouped them as they addressed my needs. Each reference has been at one time or another particularly helpful and meaningful to me. Many of these I copied and put in my journal or on the refrigerator.

God's Word is powerful and comforting. Through the Holy Spirit, these verses came alive in my times of desperate need as they never had before.

Choose one verse a day in the area you feel the greatest need. Copy it to carry with you or to post in a place where you'll see it often. Like me, you will be comforted and encouraged as you are reminded of God's timeless, loving promises.

Our Caring Lord

Old Testament

Deuteronomy 33:27	Psalm 63:5-7
Psalm 16:3	Psalm 73:25-26
Psalm 17:15	Psalm 84:11-12
Psalm 23:1	Psalm 123:1-2
Psalm 27:10	Isaiah 46:4
Psalm 34:8-10	Isaiah 54:5
Psalm 37:25	Isaiah 62:4-5
Psalm 55:22	Nahum 1:7

New Testament

Matthew 6:25-33	2 Corinthians 12:9-10
Luke 1:37, 45	Philippians 4:13 & 19
Acts 17:25, 28	1 Timothy 6:17
Romans 8:32-35	Hebrews 13:5-6
2 Corinthians 3:5	1 Peter 5:7
2 Corinthians 9:8	Revelation 7:17

Faith in Uncertainty

Old Testament

Numbers 23:19	Psalm 111:5
Deuteronomy 7:9	Psalm 112:7-8
Deuteronomy 33:27	Psalm 115:3
Joshua 21:45	Psalm 118:6-9
Joshua 23:14	Psalm 108:1
2 Chronicles 20:12	Proverbs 3:5-6
Job 42:2	Proverbs 16:20
Psalm 5:11	Isaiah 12:2

Faith in Uncertainty (cont.)

Psalm 20:7   Isaiah 25:9
Psalm 27:13   Isaiah 26:3-4
Psalm 28:6-7   Isaiah 40:8
Psalm 31:15   Isaiah 43:1-2
Psalm 33:21   Isaiah 50:10
Psalm 34:8   Jeremiah 1:19
Psalm 46:1-3   Jeremiah 32:17
Psalm 62:1-5   Daniel 4:35
Psalm 63:7   Zechariah 4:6
Psalm 91:2

New Testament

Matthew 9:22   Romans 1:17
Matthew 19:26   1 Corinthians 15:57
Mark 11:22   2 Corinthians 1:9
Luke 1:37, 45   2 Corinthians 7:4
Luke 17:5   Philippians 4:13
Luke 18:27   2 Timothy 1:12
Luke 21:33   Hebrews 10:23
John 13:7   Hebrews 11

Strength and Perseverance

Old Testament

Deuteronomy 31:6-8   Psalm 138:3
Deuteronomy 33:27   Psalm 142:3
2 Chronicles 14:11   Isaiah 12:2
Nehemiah 8:10   Isaiah 25:4
Psalm 18:32, 39   Isaiah 26:3-4
Psalm 27:1   Isaiah 27:5

Strength and Perseverance (cont.)

Psalm 28:6-7   Isaiah 40:29-31
Psalm 55:22   Isaiah 49:5
Psalm 61:1-4   Lamentations 3:25
Psalm 71:16   Daniel 10:19
Psalm 73:23-26   Nahum 1:7
Psalm 108:1   Haggai 2:4
Psalm 119:28   Zechariah 4:6

New Testament

Matthew 24:13   1 Timothy 6:12
Romans 8:23-25   2 Timothy 4:7
Romans 8:37   Hebrews 10:23
1 Corinthians 15:58   Hebrews 10:35-36
2 Corinthians 3:5   Hebrews 11
2 Corinthians 12:9-10   Hebrews 13:5-6
Galatians 6:8-10   James 5:11
Ephesians 6:10   Revelation 21:7
Philippians 4:13

Tears and Crying

Old Testament

2 Kings 22:19   Psalm 120:1
Psalm 30:5   Psalm 126:5-6
Psalm 34:17-18   Psalm 142:3
Psalm 40:1   Isaiah 25:8
Psalm 42:3-5, 11   Isaiah 38:14
Psalm 61:1-4   Isaiah 63:9
Psalm 69:2-3   Lamentations 3:54-57

Tears and Crying (cont.)

New Testament

Revelation 21:4

Rest in Times of Weariness

Old Testament

Exodus 33:14   Psalm 61:2
Deuteronomy 33:12   Psalm 63:7
Job 3:17   Psalm 73:26
Psalm 18:2   Psalm 94:19
Psalm 23:2   Isaiah 28:12
Psalm 27:14   Isaiah 30:15
Psalm 37:7   Isaiah 40:29-31

New Testament

Matthew 11:28   2 Corinthians 5:4
Romans 8:22-25   Hebrews 4:3, 9
2 Corinthians 4:16

Peace in Times of Fear

Old Testament

Genesis 50:20-21   Psalm 94:19
Deuteronomy 31:6-8   Psalm 108:1
Deuteronomy 33:27   Psalm 112:7-8
Joshua 1:9   Psalm 118:6
2 Samuel 22:2-3   Isaiah 12:2
2 Samuel 22:31-32   Isaiah 26:3-4
2 Kings 6:16   Isaiah 30:15

Peace in Times of Fear (cont.)

2 Chronicles 20:12, 17	Isaiah 35:3-4
Psalm 4:8	Isaiah 41:10
Psalm 27:1	Isaiah 43:1-3
Psalm 28:7	Jeremiah 1:19
Psalm 34:7	Lamentations 3:54-57
Psalm 46:1-3, 5	Daniel 3:17
Psalm 55:22	Daniel 10:19
Psalm 61:2	Nahum 1:7
Psalm 91:2, 4-5, 15	Zephaniah 3:15-17

New Testament

Matthew 24:6	1 Corinthians 15:57
Luke 10:41-42	Philippians 4:6-7
John 14:18, 27	Hebrews 13:5-6
John 16:33	Revelation 1:4
Romans 8:35-39	Revelation 1:17-18

Guidance

Old Testament

Genesis 50:20	Psalm 107:7
Exodus 33:14	Psalm 118:8-9
Deuteronomy 31:6	Psalm 121:5, 8
Deuteronomy 32:11-12	Psalm 142:3
Job 23:10	Psalm 143:8
Psalm 5:8	Proverbs 3:5-6
Psalm 16:11	Isaiah 43:2-3
Psalm 23:3-4	Isaiah 46:4
Psalm 25:4-5, 9, 12	Isaiah 55:8
Psalm 31:15	Isaiah 57:18

Guidance (cont.)

Psalm 32:8	Isaiah 58:11
Psalm 37:23-24	Jeremiah 10:23
Psalm 48:14	Haggai 2:4
Psalm 73:23-26	Micah 6:8
Psalm 78:53	

New Testament

Matthew 28:20	2 Timothy 3:16-17
John 16:13	Hebrews 13:5-6
Philippians 2:13	James 1:5

Trials and Hard Times

Old Testament

Genesis 41:52	Psalm 55:6, 8
Genesis 50:20	Psalm 57:1
Deuteronomy 8:2, 5-6	Psalm 61:2
Deuteronomy 33:27	Psalm 119:71
Job 23:10-11	Isaiah 38:14
Psalm 42:11	Isaiah 43:2-3
Psalm 46:1	Nahum 1:7

New Testament

John 16:33	Philippians 4:13
Romans 5:2-4	Hebrews 12:1-3
Romans 8:17-18, 28	James 1:2-4
2 Corinthians 1:3-5	1 Peter 1:3-7
2 Corinthians 4:16-18	1 Peter 2:21-23
2 Corinthians 5:2, 4	1 Peter 4:19

Trials and Hard Times (cont.)

2 Corinthians 12:9-10   Revelation 2:10
Philippians 1:23

Comfort in Times of Loneliness

Old Testament

Exodus 15:26   Psalm 63:5-6
Exodus 33:14   Psalm 73:23-25
Deuteronomy 31:8   Psalm 94:19
Deuteronomy 33:12, 27   Psalm 123:1-2
Joshua 1:5   Psalm 139:17-18
Ezra 9:9   Psalm 147:3
Psalm 23:1, 4   Isaiah 43:1-2
Psalm 27:10   Isaiah 49:15-16
Psalm 34:7   Isaiah 54:5
Psalm 46:1   Hosea 2:19
Psalm 57:1   Zephaniah 3:17
Psalm 61:1-4

New Testament

Matthew 28:20   2 Corinthians 1:3-5
John 14:16, 18   1 Thessalonians 4:17-18
John 14:26, 27   2 Thessalonians 2:16-17
Romans 8:26-27   Hebrews 13:5-6
Romans 8:38-39   1 Peter 5:7

Hope and Eternal Perspective

Old Testament

Deuteronomy 33:27   Isaiah 25:8-9

Hope and Eternal Perspective (cont.)

2 Samuel 22:31-32   Isaiah 55:8-9
Job 3:17   Isaiah 60:20
Psalm 17:15   Isaiah 64:1, 4
Psalm 18:2   Jeremiah 3:23
Psalm 42:11   Jeremiah 17:7
Psalm 46:5   Daniel 4:35
Psalm 62:1, 5   Micah 2:12
Psalm 115:3   Malachi 3:6
Psalm 130:5-6

New Testament

Luke 1:37, 45   Colossians 3:2
Luke 21:33   1 Thessalonians 4:16-18
John 13:7   2 Timothy 1:12
John 16:33   Titus 2:13
Romans 5:2-5   Hebrews 4:9
Romans 8:22-25   Hebrews 10:34, 37
Romans 8:28   Hebrews 11
Romans 8:38-39   Hebrews 12:1-2
Romans 15:13   Hebrews 13:8, 14
1 Corinthians 15:57   1 Peter 1:3-8, 13
2 Corinthians 4:16-18   2 Peter 3:13
2 Corinthians 5:4-5   Revelation 4:11
Philippians 1:23   Revelation 7:14-17
Philippians 3:20-21   Revelation 21:1-5
Colossians 1:5

Pouring Out Your Heart to God

Old Testament

1 Samuel 3:9	Psalm 63:5-6
2 Chronicles 14:11	Psalm 65:2
Job 5:8	Psalm 66:18
Psalm 10:17	Psalm 73:25
Psalm 22:11, 19, 24	Psalm 86:5
Psalm 28:6-7	Psalm 91:15
Psalm 35:1-2	Psalm 116:1-4
Psalm 37:5	Psalm 123:1-2
Psalm 38:9	Psalm 139:23-24
Psalm 50:15	Psalm 145:18-19
Psalm 55:22	Isaiah 58:9
Psalm 61:1-4	Isaiah 65:24

New Testament

Matthew 6:5-15	Hebrews 4:16
Mark 11:25	James 1:5-7
Romans 8:26-27	James 5:13, 16
Philippians 4:6-7	1 Peter 5:7

Forgiving and Letting Go

Old Testament

Genesis 41:52	Genesis 50:20

New Testament

Matthew 6:14-15	Ephesians 4:32
Matthew 18:15-22	Colossians 3:12-13
Mark 11:25	1 Peter 2:20-23
Ephesians 4:26	

Appendix D

A Bear with a Badge

Hurry up! We're going to be late!" I yelled impatiently at my four-year-old son as I snatched him up and almost threw him into the car.

The last few months were a nightmare. I kept hoping I would wake up to find it was all just a bad dream. Without warning, my husband of thirteen years abandoned me for a younger woman. My world came crashing down. I was shattered. Barely surviving. The concept of even beginning to pick up the pieces was as far away as God. Or so it seemed.

I had always believed in God and his love through Jesus. Where was He now? Where was all that love? I felt all alone fighting for my life and for my son. Where was justice? Fairness? Right triumphing over wrong?

That night I was taking Danny to spend the weekend with his dad. Every time I left my little boy, it ripped my heart out. I dreaded the unbearable grief and agony. Little did I know that this particular evening would be different.

On the way we made a brief stop at the mall. As we left, my son squealed with delight when he saw a sheriff's car parked out front. He ran toward it quivering with excitement. The deputy greeted us with a warm smile. "I am Deputy Randy."

Knowing every little boy's heart, he asked him if he would like to sit behind the wheel. Propped up on his knees, he gripped the steering wheel and made *vroom vroom* noises. Then the deputy let him turn on the bright red flashing lights. Danny beamed with ecstasy. My heart melted.

After helping him climb out, the deputy opened the trunk, eyes twinkling and said, "I have something for you." He lifted out a big brown teddy bear with a sheriff's badge.

Stooping down, he looked into Danny's eyes and said, "This is for you because you are such a good boy."

All I can recall after that was fighting back the tears, driving in silence, as my little boy sat next to me clutching that big brown bear.

Leaving him that night was just as painful, but somehow my burden seemed lighter and a little more bearable.

The next day I sent a thank you note:

Dear Deputy Randy,
You will never know how much your kindness touched my son and me last night. Danny's father left and we are in the deepest, darkest valley we have ever known. The way you reached out to my little boy will never be forgotten. And the big brown bear will always be a treasure to him. Thank you for letting God use you to give us hope.

As I wrote that letter, I realized that God *was* there. He had been all along. Only I just wasn't looking. He showed his love through this person in a way that He knew we needed. In a language a four-year-old could understand.

Now many years later, I have learned that one way God loves us is through other people. And now that many of my broken pieces have mended, I want to be one who pours out His love to someone else in pain.

For the last sixteen years, that deputy remembered Danny with cards and gifts and visits . . . even a ride-along. My son is now twenty. He has graduated from the Police Cadet Academy, and is working toward his college degree.

Guess what is still sitting on his bed?